Pharma's Pulse Leading With Heart In Indian Healthcare

AF519979

Verses Kindler Publication

Verses Kindler Publication.
Website: www.verseskindlerpublication.com

© Copyright, 2024, Mr. Jitendra Kumar Sharma
All rights reserved. No part of this book may be reproduced, stored in a retrieval system, or transmitted, in any form by any means, electronic, mechanical, magnetic, Optical, chemical, manual, photocopying, recording or otherwise, without the prior Written consent of its Writer.

Pharma's Pulse Leading With Heart In Indian Healthcare

By: Mr. Jitendra Kumar Sharma
ISBN: 978-93-5605-844-6
SELF-HELP 1st Edition

Price: INR 350 / $18

The opinions/ contents expressed in this book are solely of the author and do not represent the opinions/ standings/ Thoughts of PUBLISHER.

DISCLAIMER

This book is written by Jitendra Kumar Sharma.

The published work is the original contents of the author and has done her best to edit and make it plagiarism free.

The characters may be fictitious or based on real events but they are not meant to hurt anyone's feeling nor portray anything against any caste or system.

In case of any plagiarized write-up the author is solely responsible for it. The publisher would not be responsible for it.

Author Jitendra Kumar Sharma receiving Business excellence award along with co- founder of Aster Medipharm Mr. Pawan Kumar Pareek at New Delhi.

Table of Contents

Chapter 1

Introduction: Unveiling the Heartbeat of Indian Pharma

I have been a part of the Indian Pharmaceutical Industry for almost 2 decades now and I have observed the industry's growth, ups and downs, and the innovations in the industry very closely.

As of 14th May 2024, the pharmaceutical industry in India is currently valued at $50 billion. It is expected to reach $60 billion by the end of 2024.

Indian Pharmaceutical industry is the 3rd largest in the world by volume and 11th largest by value.

India's first pharmaceutical company was established in 1901. Since then, the Indian pharmaceutical industry has emerged as the cornerstone of the country's healthcare system and has played an important role in making medicines available at affordable prices not only in India but the whole world.

The Indian pharmaceutical industry has a rich history dating back many years. Our industry has witnessed and witnessed phenomenal growth and development. Many positive factors contribute to this growth such as strong domestic demand, a skilled workforce, favorable government policies, and a strong focus on research and innovation.

I will try to summarize the origin and the development of pharmaceutical industry in India so far:

1. Early onset and development

The roots of India's pharmaceutical industry can be traced back to the early 20th century when a few entrepreneurial pioneers laid the foundation for what would eventually become one of the country's most important industries. During the period of independence, Indian pharmaceutical companies had mainly focused on the production of basic drugs and pharmaceutical products to meet the domestic demand.

However, the industry faced many challenges during this period, including limited raw material availability, obsolete products, and regulatory barriers imposed by colonial authorities. Despite these obstacles, a handful of visionary leaders persevered, laying the groundwork for the industry's future growth and expansion.

2. Growth and expansion

After independence in 1947, the Indian pharmaceutical industry witnessed a period of rapid growth and expansion, driven by a combination of government subsidies, technological advances, and increased demand for expensive drugs.

The establishment of institutions such as the Pharmaceutical Council of India and the National Pharmacy have helped in standardizing pharmaceutical protocols and improving quality control standards

A major milestone in the development trajectory of the industry was the introduction of the Patents Act in 1970, which patented pharmaceutical products and allowed for generic drug development. This landmark legislation democratized access to medicines, making essential and more affordable medicines and become accessible to millions across India and beyond.

3. Global Leadership and Innovation

Today, the Indian pharmaceutical industry stands as a global leader in generic medicines, catering to a significant portion of the world's demand for essential medicines. Indian pharmaceutical companies have earned a reputation for their ability to develop cost-effective formulations, high-quality products, and dedication to product innovation.

The industry's contribution to medical innovation is significant. Indian companies are actively engaged in R&D in a wide range of therapeutic areas including oncology, cardiovascular diseases, and infectious diseases. Since the pioneering development of low-cost antiretroviral drugs for the treatment of HIV/AIDS, from AIDS treatment to biosimilars and specialty drug development, Indian pharmaceutical companies across the globe have been at the forefront of medical breakthroughs for the benefit of patients.

4. Providing Affordable Healthcare Solutions

One of the key characteristics of the Indian pharmaceutical industry is its commitment to providing affordable healthcare solutions to people across socio-economic levels. Through the scale of economies, innovation, and robust supply chains, pharmaceutical companies have been able to produce quality drugs at a fraction of the cost compared to their counterparts in the West

This focus on affordability has not only transformed healthcare flows in India but has also made Indian pharmaceutical companies key players in global healthcare initiatives. Being a provider of life-saving medicines for infectious diseases, chronic conditions, and rare diseases, Indian pharmaceutical companies play a vital role in accessing and dispensing vital medicines to millions of people around the world improving health outcomes.

The journey of the Indian pharmaceutical industry from its humble beginnings to its current status as a global leader is a testament to its leadership and entrepreneurial vision, innovation, and resilience. By providing affordable healthcare solutions, stimulating medical innovation, and shaping global healthcare initiatives, the Indian pharmaceutical industry continues to have a profound impact on the lives of people around the world.

Let me tell you an interesting fact (if you don't already know), India is often referred to as the "Pharmacy of the world" due to its reputation as a leading producer of generic medicines and because it provides it worldwide. Our country's pharmaceutical industry is a large part of the global pharmaceutical market. The Indian pharmaceutical industry has a diverse portfolio of products including antibiotics, cardiovascular drugs, vaccines, and cancer treatments.

The key strength of our business is our ability to produce quality medicines at a fraction of the cost of our counterparts in developed countries. Besides making healthcare affordable for millions of patients within India, costs have made Indian pharmaceutical companies major players in supplying essential medicines to developing countries around the world.

Initially, the Indian pharmaceutical industry was known for its proficiency in the development of synthetic drugs, it has focused heavily on innovation and research. Many Indian companies have been involved in innovative drugs and actively developing bio like drugs, contributing to the advancement of medical science and technology.

The industry's emphasis on generic drug manufacturing has contributed significantly to improving access to essential medicines, especially in developing countries. By building medicines and offering affordable patented alternatives, Indian pharmaceutical companies play a vital role in making healthcare accessible and affordable for millions across the globe.

The regulatory framework governing the Indian pharmaceutical industry has undergone significant reforms over the years, in line with international standards and best practices. Regulatory agencies such as the Central Drugs Standard Control Organization (CDSCO) ensure that drugs manufactured in India meet stringent quality and safety standards.

The Indian pharmaceutical industry is the backbone of the country's healthcare system. Its extensive network of manufacturing plants, research centers, and distribution channels ensures a continuous supply of vital medicines to healthcare providers across the country

Apart from its health impact, the pharmaceutical industry contributes significantly to the Indian economy. It creates employment opportunities, fosters innovation, and generates remittances, thus playing an important role in the country's economic growth and development

Despite the achievements, the Indian pharmaceutical industry faces various challenges such as regulatory challenges, increasing competition, and the need for continuous innovation but these challenges present opportunities for growth, innovation, and further expansion in the global market.

The Indian pharmaceutical industry stands as a beacon of innovation, affordability, and availability in healthcare. Excellence in healthcare is not only required in India, but it also positively impacts the lives of millions of people worldwide, making it an important part of the global healthcare landscape.

The future of the pharmaceutical industry in India looks very bright and promising but we still have a long way to go. And one of the key elements that shouldn't be overlooked in this scenario is the need for compassionate leaders who are well-versed in technology and medical science. At the same time, they should understand the importance and impact they have on their team. Because no matter how evolved we become in science and technology, if we lack the correct leadership, we will not be able to capitalize on our potential. We need leaders who people should want to follow and listen to. We need leaders who understand the great responsibility they have along with great power as a leader.

Leadership Style and Philosophy in the Indian Pharmaceutical Industry

Leadership in the Indian pharmaceutical industry is multifaceted. It reflects the traditional hierarchical structures and modern management strategies that meet the evolving needs of the industry. Let's delve into the various leadership styles prevalent in the Indian pharmaceutical context, examine the characteristics and characteristics of effective pharmaceutical leaders, and discuss the importance of leadership development and policy development to ensure the continued growth and sustainability of the industry.

1. Traditional Hierarchical Models vs. Contemporary Approaches

In the past, leaders in the Indian pharmaceutical industry tended to follow a traditional hierarchy. It was characterized by top-down decision-making and a rigid organizational structure. However, as the industry has evolved, there has been a shift towards more modern methods. These methods and models emphasize collaboration, innovation, and employee empowerment.

Modern medical leaders understand the importance of fostering a culture of openness and transparency. Ideas are encouraged to flow freely, and employees are empowered to take ownership of their work. This shift towards an inclusive leadership style reflects the changing dynamics of the industry, where agility and flexibility are essential to succeed in a rapidly changing global marketplace

2. Characteristics of Effective Pharmaceutical Leaders

Effective pharmaceutical leaders have a unique and distinctive quality. These qualities set them apart in a competitive and challenging industry. These characteristics include:

- **Strategic vision:** Pharmaceutical leaders must have a clear vision for the future of their organizations. They must have a keen interest in understanding market trends, regulatory developments, and technological developments. They must be able to anticipate challenges and opportunities and create a strategy for long-term success.
- **Integrity and ethics:** Integrity is a non-negotiable in the pharmaceutical industry, where patient safety and trust are paramount. Effective leaders lead by example, demonstrating integrity, transparency, and a commitment to making sound and ethical decisions in all aspects of their work.
- **Adaptability:** The pharmaceutical industry is constantly evolving, with new technologies, regulatory changes, and market developments shaping the landscape. Effective leaders must be flexible and agile. They should be able to adapt quickly to respond to changing circumstances and seize emerging opportunities.

3. Importance of Leadership Development and Succession Planning

Leadership development and succession programs are essential to ensure long-term growth and development in a dynamic and competitive sector such as pharmaceuticals. Organizations should invest in the development of the next generation of leaders.

It is the responsibility of the organization to provide the necessary skills, knowledge, and experience to successfully overcome the challenges of the project.

Leadership development programs should be tailored to the specific needs and challenges of the pharmaceutical industry, and provide opportunities for mentoring, coaching, and hands-on experiences for aspiring leaders. Follow-up arrangements ensure continuity of leadership and fewer obstacles during a transition period. This enables organizations to maintain growth and continue to improve.

Leadership style and philosophy play an important role in the success and strategy of the Indian pharmaceutical industry. Effective leadership must embody qualities such as strategic vision, integrity, and flexibility while prioritizing leadership development and succession planning to ensure continuous business growth and it will continue to be there for years to come.

To develop effective leadership in the pharmaceutical industry, we need leaders with a deep understanding of the scientific challenges of pharmaceutical research and the dynamic business environment in which companies operate.

We need leaders who take a multifaceted approach that balances scientific expertise with strategic acumen, business acumen, and a strong commitment to ethical principles. We're dealing with health care here, so it's very important for leaders to be ethical.

The Need for Compassionate Leadership

Compassionate leadership emerges as an important guiding principle for navigating the unique challenges and opportunities faced by business leaders in the fast-paced dynamic environment of the Indian pharmaceutical industry. Let us understand the importance and significance of compassionate leadership in the Indian pharmaceutical industry, and explore its role in promoting innovation, ethical decision-making, and employee engagement involvement, along with well-being.

Compassionate leadership goes beyond traditional concepts of authority and command, emphasizing empathy, understanding, and concern for the well-being of others. At its core, compassionate leadership is about embracing humanity in each individual and fostering a culture of caring, support, and collaboration in organizations.

In the Indian pharmaceutical industry where the stakes are high and the challenges are complex, compassionate leadership is crucial. Not only should leaders navigate complex regulations, market competition, and public health problems but also ensure that their decisions and actions reflect a genuine commitment to the well-being of patients, staff, and the wider community.

1. Challenges and Opportunities Faced by Pharmaceutical Leaders in India

Pharmacy leaders in India face many challenges. These challenges range from regulatory barriers to price pressures to market competition and public health concerns. Regulatory challenges in particular pose significant challenges for business leaders, who must navigate the complexity of laws, regulations, and compliance requirements.

Moreover, the Indian pharmaceutical industry operates in a highly competitive environment, both domestically and globally. Today, innovation, cost, and quality are paramount. Leaders should always strive to differentiate their organizations and products while also ensuring that they adhere to ethical standards and best practices.

Despite these challenges, the Indian pharmaceutical industry offers ample opportunities for growth and development. With greater demographic diversity, growing healthcare needs, and growing government policies to promote access to and affordability of healthcare, there is tremendous potential for innovation, expansion, and availability influence in the project.

2. Role of Compassionate Leadership in Fostering Innovation and Ethical Decision-Making

Compassionate leadership plays an important role in promoting innovation and promoting ethical decision-making in the Indian pharmaceutical industry. By fostering a culture of trust, collaboration, and psychological safety, compassionate leaders empower employees to think creatively, take calculated risks, and execute ideas if it's a bold move that could change the backbone of health care.

Furthermore, compassionate leaders prioritize ethical considerations in all aspects of their decision-making, recognizing the tremendous impact their actions have on patients, healthcare professionals, and society. They lead by example, demonstrating honesty, transparency, and commitment to ethics even in the face of difficult choices or competing interests.

3. Promoting Employee Engagement and Well-Being

In addition to promoting innovation and ethical decision-making, compassionate leadership is essential to enhance employee engagement, satisfaction, and well-being. Leaders who demonstrate care, empathy, and appreciation for their employees provide a positive working environment in which individuals feel valued, supported, and motivated to behave at their best.

By prioritizing the physical, emotional, and operational well-being of their employees, compassionate leaders foster a culture of flexibility, collaboration, and continuous improvement within their organizations This improves productivity, retention, and within the organization overall effort increases. Ultimately this accounts for the long-term and sustainable success of Indian medicine.

Compassionate leadership is not only a desirable trait but also a critical ingredient for success in Indian medicine. By infusing empathy, understanding, and caring, medical leaders can address challenges, seize opportunities, and have a positive impact that extends beyond the boundaries of their organizations.

We explored the concept of compassionate leadership and its importance in Indian medicine. We talked about how compassionate leadership supports innovation, drives ethical decisions, promotes employee engagement and well-being, and ultimately defines pharmaceutical organization culture and success.

As we conclude this chapter, I encourage you, dear readers, to delve deeper into the subsequent chapters of this book. In the coming chapters, we will examine and discuss the principles and practices of compassionate leadership and their application in the Indian pharmaceutical industry. By raising awareness of the critical role compassionate leaders play in creating positive change and sustainable success, we can work together to build a brighter future for healthcare in India and beyond.

Join me as we continue our journey into the heart of Indian pharma, where leadership meets compassion, and together, we set the stage for change towards a healthier, more compassionate world.

Chapter 2

Understanding leadership

Whenever we hear the word "leader", our mind paints the picture of a person who is competent, knows what he does, is responsible, and knows how to handle and guide their team with ease.

Leadership is and has always been an important aspect not only in healthcare but all sectors. With new generations coming into the workforce, the leaders and leadership styles have changed over time. There used to be a time when leaders, especially in healthcare used to dedicate their whole lives to the work. They barely took time for their personal lives. This is changing with time as the newer generation wants a work-life balance for themselves. They realize that their work is not their whole life but a part of their life. An important part for sure but only one part of life.

When it comes to the definition of good leadership, it is subjective depending upon the point of view of individuals.

For some, leadership is about projecting your power in such a way that people follow you. For others, leadership is collaborating with your team and working towards achieving your goals.

There are many theories and definitions of leadership and a leader out there, each with its own take on a leader and leadership qualities.

According to me, an effective leader is one who leads by example for their team.

Leadership in the pharmaceutical industry, particularly within the Indian context, involves a nuanced blend of strategic vision, ethical integrity, adaptability, empathy, and a commitment to innovation. These characteristics are vital for navigating the unique challenges and opportunities presented by the sector. Effective leadership in this industry not only drives profitability but also ensures that companies contribute positively to public health, uphold ethical standards, and foster a culture of continuous improvement and innovation.

Let me try to sum up the characteristics, an effective pharmaceutical leader must possess.

1. Visionary Thinking

Visionary Thinking is paramount for leaders in the Indian pharmaceutical industry. In a rapidly evolving market, leaders must possess a clear and forward-looking vision that guides their company's trajectory. This involves anticipating future trends in healthcare, such as demographic shifts, emerging diseases, advancements in biotechnology, and changes in regulatory landscapes.

For instance, visionary leaders in Indian pharma are those who foresaw the potential of generic drugs when many companies were focused on branded formulations. This foresight allowed India to become a global leader in generic medicine production. Visionary leaders also recognize the importance of expanding into biopharmaceuticals and biosimilars, anticipating the growing demand for these advanced therapies.

Furthermore, visionary thinking involves setting long-term goals and creating strategies to achieve them. Leaders must balance immediate business needs with strategic initiatives that ensure sustainable growth. They need to communicate their vision effectively to inspire and align their teams, fostering a shared sense of purpose and direction.

2. Integrity

Integrity is a cornerstone of effective leadership in the pharmaceutical sector. The nature of this industry, which directly impacts public health, necessitates the highest levels of ethical conduct. Leaders must ensure that their decisions and actions uphold honesty, transparency, and fairness.

In the Indian context, where the pharmaceutical industry has occasionally faced scrutiny over issues such as drug quality, pricing, and regulatory compliance, maintaining integrity is crucial. Ethical leadership involves making tough decisions that prioritize patient safety and well-being over short-term profits. For example, during the COVID-19 pandemic, several Indian pharmaceutical companies committed to producing affordable vaccines and treatments, demonstrating integrity and social responsibility.

Integrity also extends to transparent business practices. Leaders must foster a culture where ethical conduct is rewarded, and any deviations are addressed promptly and fairly. This includes ensuring compliance with local and international regulations, accurately reporting financial and operational data, and engaging in fair marketing practices.

3. Adaptability

Adaptability is essential for leaders in the pharmaceutical industry due to its dynamic nature. The sector is subject to frequent changes driven by regulatory updates, scientific advancements, market competition, and public health needs. Leaders must be flexible and resilient, capable of navigating these shifts while keeping their organizations stable and forward-moving.

Regulatory changes, for instance, can significantly impact pharmaceutical operations. Leaders need to stay informed about regulatory developments and be prepared to adapt their strategies accordingly. This might involve reformulating products to meet new standards, adjusting supply chains, or modifying marketing approaches.

Scientific advancements also require adaptable leadership. With ongoing research leading to new treatments and technologies, leaders must be open to adopting these innovations and integrating them into their product portfolios. This may involve investing in new research and development (R&D) capabilities, forming strategic partnerships, or acquiring emerging biotech firms.

Market dynamics, such as increased competition from global players or changes in consumer preferences, further necessitate adaptability. Leaders must be agile, and able to pivot strategies to maintain competitive advantages. For example, embracing digital transformation in marketing and sales, leveraging data analytics for better decision-making, or entering new markets to diversify revenue streams.

4. Empathy

Empathy is a critical trait for leaders in the pharmaceutical industry. Understanding the needs and concerns of patients, employees, and other stakeholders is essential for making informed and compassionate decisions. Empathetic leaders foster a positive organizational culture, enhance employee engagement, and improve patient outcomes.

In the Indian pharmaceutical industry, empathy can manifest in various ways. Leaders might prioritize patient-centric approaches in their business strategies, ensuring that their products are not only effective but also accessible and affordable. This could involve implementing tiered pricing models, providing financial assistance programs, or engaging in community health initiatives.

For employees, empathetic leadership means creating a supportive work environment where staff feel valued and heard. This includes promoting work-life balance, offering professional development opportunities, and maintaining open lines of communication. By understanding and addressing the needs of their employees, leaders can enhance job satisfaction and productivity, which ultimately benefits the organization.

Stakeholders, including healthcare providers, regulators, and shareholders, also benefit from empathetic leadership. Leaders who actively listen to and consider the perspectives of these groups can build stronger, more collaborative relationships. This can lead to more effective regulatory compliance, better market positioning, and increased trust and loyalty from stakeholders.

5. Innovation

Innovation is indispensable for staying competitive in the pharmaceutical industry. Leaders must encourage a culture of innovation, where new ideas are welcomed, and continuous improvement is the norm. This is particularly important in India, where the pharmaceutical market is highly competitive and rapidly evolving.

Supporting R&D is a key aspect of fostering innovation. Leaders must allocate resources to research projects, ensuring that their teams have the tools and funding needed to explore new treatments and technologies. This might involve establishing dedicated R&D centers, collaborating with academic institutions, or participating in government-funded research initiatives.

Encouraging a culture of innovation also means promoting creativity and risk-taking within the organization. Leaders should create an environment where employees feel empowered to suggest new ideas and experiment with novel approaches. This could involve implementing innovation programs, holding regular brainstorming sessions, and recognizing and rewarding innovative contributions.

Innovation is not limited to product development. It can also encompass process improvements, such as streamlining manufacturing operations, adopting advanced technologies like artificial intelligence and machine learning for drug discovery, and enhancing supply chain efficiencies. Leaders who prioritize innovation in all aspects of their business are better positioned to meet the evolving needs of the healthcare market.

Effective leadership in the Indian pharmaceutical industry requires a combination of visionary thinking, integrity, adaptability, empathy, and a commitment to innovation. These characteristics enable leaders to navigate the unique challenges of the sector, drive their companies toward sustainable growth, and make a positive impact on public health. By fostering a culture that values ethical conduct, continuous improvement, and compassionate decision-making, leaders can ensure that their organizations not only succeed but also contribute meaningfully to society. As the industry continues to evolve, the importance of these leadership qualities will only grow, underscoring the need for leaders who are prepared to meet the challenges and opportunities of the future.

Leadership Styles in Indian Pharma

The Indian pharmaceutical industry is a dynamic and complex sector that requires diverse leadership styles to navigate its unique challenges and opportunities. As discussed, leaders in this industry must balance the demands of business performance with ethical responsibilities, innovation, regulatory compliance, and employee engagement. Several leadership styles can be observed within the Indian pharmaceutical industry, each bringing distinct advantages and potential drawbacks. Let us explore four prominent leadership styles: transformational, transactional, servant, and participative leadership, and examine how these styles can be effectively applied in the context of Indian pharma.

1. Transformational Leadership

Transformational leadership is characterized by the ability to inspire and motivate employees to exceed their own expectations and achieve extraordinary results. Transformational leaders create a vision for the future, communicate it compellingly, and engage their teams in working towards that vision. This style is particularly effective in fostering innovation and driving organizational change.

In the Indian pharmaceutical industry, transformational leaders play a crucial role in navigating the rapidly evolving landscape. They encourage a culture of continuous improvement and innovation, which is essential for staying competitive in a market where new technologies and scientific advancements are constantly emerging.

These leaders are adept at identifying opportunities for growth and driving initiatives that lead to the development of new products, processes, and markets.

Transformational leaders in Indian pharma also focus on the growth and development of their employees. They recognize that the success of their organization depends on the capabilities and engagement of their workforce. By providing mentorship, training, and opportunities for professional development, they help employees achieve their full potential. This not only enhances employee satisfaction and retention but also builds a talent pipeline that supports the company's long-term success.

An example of transformational leadership in Indian pharma can be seen in Dr. Kiran Mazumdar-Shaw, the founder of Biocon. Under her leadership, Biocon has grown from a small industrial enzymes company to one of India's leading biotechnology firms. Dr. Mazumdar-Shaw's visionary leadership, commitment to innovation, and focus on employee development have been instrumental in Biocon's success. She has also been a strong advocate for affordable healthcare, reflecting the broader impact that transformational leaders can have on society.

2. Transactional Leadership

Transactional leadership is based on structured tasks and clear rewards or penalties based on performance. This style focuses on maintaining order, achieving specific goals, and ensuring that employees meet predefined standards. While it may not always encourage innovation or employee satisfaction, transactional leadership can be effective in certain situations, such as managing routine operations, ensuring compliance with regulations, and achieving short-term objectives.

In the Indian pharmaceutical industry, transactional leadership is often seen in roles that require strict adherence to regulatory standards and operational efficiency. For instance, the production and quality control functions in pharmaceutical manufacturing are areas where transactional leadership can be highly effective. Leaders in these roles need to ensure that products are manufactured according to stringent quality standards and regulatory requirements. Clear guidelines, performance metrics, and a system of rewards and penalties help maintain high standards and ensure compliance.

Transactional leaders also play a crucial role in managing large-scale operations and complex supply chains. They focus on optimizing processes, reducing costs, and improving efficiency. By setting clear expectations and holding employees accountable for their performance, transactional leaders can achieve significant improvements in operational effectiveness.

However, the limitations of transactional leadership should be acknowledged. While it can ensure consistency and reliability in routine tasks, it may not foster the creativity and innovation needed for long-term growth. Employees may also feel less engaged and motivated if they perceive their work as purely transactional without opportunities for personal growth and development.

3. Servant Leadership

Servant leadership prioritizes the needs of employees and other stakeholders, emphasizing the leader's role as a servant to their team. This style is characterized by humility, empathy, and a strong commitment to serving others. Servant leaders focus on creating a supportive environment where employees feel valued, empowered, and motivated to contribute their best efforts.

In the Indian pharmaceutical industry, servant leadership can have a profound impact on organizational culture and employee engagement. By putting the needs of employees first, servant leaders build trust and loyalty, which can lead to higher levels of job satisfaction and productivity. This leadership style is particularly effective in fostering a collaborative and inclusive work environment, where employees feel comfortable sharing ideas and taking initiative.

Servant leadership also aligns well with the ethical responsibilities of the pharmaceutical industry. By prioritizing the well-being of employees, patients, and the broader community, servant leaders can build a reputation for integrity and social responsibility. This can enhance the company's brand image and strengthen relationships with stakeholders, including regulators, healthcare providers, and patients.

4. Participative Leadership

Participative leadership, also known as democratic leadership, involves seeking input from team members and making decisions collaboratively. This style emphasizes the value of diverse perspectives and encourages employees to contribute to the decision-making process. Participative leadership can lead to higher employee engagement, more creative solutions, and a stronger sense of ownership and commitment among team members.

In the Indian pharmaceutical industry, participative leadership is particularly beneficial in areas that require complex problem-solving and innovation. By involving employees in decision-making, leaders can tap into a wide range of knowledge, skills, and experiences. This collaborative approach can lead to more innovative solutions and better decision-making, as employees feel empowered to share their insights and ideas.

Participative leadership also promotes a culture of transparency and accountability. When employees are involved in decisions that affect their work, they are more likely to understand the rationale behind those decisions and take ownership of the outcomes. This can lead to higher levels of motivation, job satisfaction, and overall performance.

One example of participative leadership in Indian pharma is Dr. Ajay Piramal, chairman of Piramal Group. Dr. Piramal is known for his inclusive leadership style, encouraging open communication and collaboration across all levels of the organization. Under his leadership, Piramal Group has fostered a culture of innovation and continuous improvement, leveraging the collective expertise of its employees to drive business success.

Balancing Leadership Styles

While each of these leadership styles has its strengths, the most effective leaders in the Indian pharmaceutical industry often employ a combination of these approaches, tailored to the specific needs of their organization and the challenges they face. For instance, a leader might adopt a transformational approach to drive innovation and strategic growth, while also using transactional methods to ensure compliance and operational efficiency. Similarly, servant leadership principles can be integrated with participative practices to create a supportive and collaborative work environment.

Effective leaders are those who can adapt their style to different situations and contexts, recognizing that no single approach is sufficient to address the complexities of the pharmaceutical industry. By understanding and leveraging the strengths of various leadership styles, leaders can create a balanced and dynamic approach that drives organizational success while upholding ethical standards and fostering a positive impact on public health.

The Indian pharmaceutical industry requires leaders who can navigate a complex and rapidly changing landscape with a combination of visionary thinking, integrity, adaptability, empathy, and a commitment to innovation. Transformational, transactional, servant, and participative leadership styles each offer unique advantages and can be effectively applied to different aspects of the industry. By adopting a flexible and balanced approach, leaders can drive their organizations towards sustainable growth, ethical excellence, and a positive impact on society.

Historical Examples and Case Studies from Indian Healthcare Leaders Who Exemplified Leadership Principles

Leadership in the Indian pharmaceutical industry has often been marked by visionaries who combine strategic thinking with a deep sense of ethics and a commitment to public health. The following case studies highlight how some of India's most influential healthcare leaders have exemplified key leadership principles, driving both business success and significant advancements in public health.

1. Dr. Yusuf Hamied - Cipla

Dr. Yusuf Hamied, the chairman of Cipla, stands out as a beacon of visionary leadership combined with ethical integrity. His contributions have not only transformed Cipla but also had a profound impact on global healthcare, particularly in the fight against HIV/AIDS.

Visionary Thinking and Ethical Leadership

In the early 2000s, the HIV/AIDS epidemic was causing widespread devastation across Africa, but the cost of antiretroviral drugs was prohibitively high for many affected countries. Pharmaceutical giants held patents on these drugs, keeping prices out of reach for millions of patients. Dr. Hamied saw an opportunity to address this crisis by leveraging Cipla's capabilities in generic drug manufacturing.

In a move that was both bold and compassionate, Dr. Hamied decided to produce generic versions of these life-saving drugs at a fraction of the cost of the branded versions. This decision was not merely a business strategy but a humanitarian effort driven by a commitment to making essential medicines accessible to all. By challenging the status quo and prioritizing patient needs over profits, Dr. Hamied set a new standard for the pharmaceutical industry.

Impact on Global Health

Dr. Hamied's decision to offer antiretroviral drugs at $1 per day was groundbreaking. It dramatically lowered the cost of HIV treatment, making it accessible to millions of people in developing countries. This initiative played a critical role in transforming the global response to the HIV/AIDS epidemic, saving countless lives, and demonstrating the power of ethical leadership.

Moreover, Cipla's success under Dr. Hamied's leadership showcased the potential of Indian pharmaceutical companies to compete on the global stage while adhering to high ethical standards. His legacy continues to inspire leaders in the industry to pursue business goals that align with broader social responsibilities.

2. Dr. K. Anji Reddy - Dr. Reddy's Laboratories

Dr. K. Anji Reddy, the visionary founder of Dr. Reddy's Laboratories, exemplifies leadership that combines innovation with a relentless pursuit of excellence. His commitment to making high-quality medicines affordable and accessible has left an indelible mark on the pharmaceutical industry.

Innovation and Research

Dr. Reddy's leadership was characterized by his unwavering belief in the power of innovation. He was one of the first Indian pharmaceutical entrepreneurs to invest heavily in research and development (R&D). At a time when the industry was primarily focused on generic drugs, Dr. Reddy saw the potential for Indian companies to innovate and create new treatments.

Under his guidance, Dr. Reddy's Laboratories made significant strides in R&D, leading to the development of several breakthrough drugs. His emphasis on innovation helped the company transition from a domestic player to a global leader in pharmaceuticals. Dr. Reddy's vision extended beyond business success; he aimed to transform healthcare by providing high-quality, affordable medicines to people around the world.

Commitment to Accessibility

Dr. Reddy's commitment to making medicines affordable was evident in his company's pricing strategies and business practices. He believed that profitability should not come at the expense of accessibility. This ethos was reflected in the company's efforts to produce cost-effective generic drugs and innovative therapies that addressed unmet medical needs.

One notable example of Dr. Reddy's leadership was his focus on the development of generic versions of complex, high-cost medications. This strategy not only made essential treatments more affordable but also positioned Dr. Reddy's Laboratories as a pioneer in the field of generic pharmaceuticals.

3. Pankaj Patel - Zydus Cadila

Pankaj Patel, the chairman of Zydus Cadila, has demonstrated a unique blend of strategic vision and a deep commitment to innovation and public health. His leadership has been instrumental in transforming Zydus Cadila into a global pharmaceutical and healthcare leader.

Strategic Vision

Pankaj Patel's strategic vision has been a driving force behind Zydus Cadila's growth and success. He has consistently focused on expanding the company's capabilities through strategic investments in research and development, as well as acquisitions that complement and enhance the company's portfolio.

Under Patel's leadership, Zydus Cadila has made significant advances in biotechnology and vaccine development. His foresight in recognizing the importance of these fields has positioned the company at the forefront of scientific innovation. This strategic approach has not only strengthened Zydus Cadila's market position but also contributed to advancements in healthcare.

Innovation in Vaccine Development

One of the most notable achievements under Patel's leadership was the development of the world's first indigenously developed DNA plasmid vaccine for COVID-19. This groundbreaking achievement demonstrated Zydus Cadila's innovative capabilities and highlighted

Patel's commitment to addressing global health challenges through cutting-edge research and development.

The COVID-19 vaccine, known as ZyCoV-D, represented a significant milestone in the fight against the pandemic. It showcased the potential of Indian pharmaceutical companies to develop advanced biotechnological solutions and reinforced the importance of innovation in addressing public health crises. Patel's leadership during this critical period exemplified how strategic vision and innovation can drive meaningful contributions to global health.

4. Dilip Shanghvi - Sun Pharmaceuticals

Dilip Shanghvi, the founder of Sun Pharmaceuticals, is renowned for his exceptional leadership and strategic acumen. His ability to identify growth opportunities and drive operational excellence has been instrumental in building one of the largest pharmaceutical companies in India.

Strategic Acquisitions and Growth

Shanghvi's leadership style is characterized by a focus on strategic growth through acquisitions and operational efficiency. One of the most significant moves in Sun Pharmaceuticals' history was the acquisition of Ranbaxy Laboratories in 2014. This bold decision significantly expanded the company's global footprint and market share, making it one of the world's largest specialty generic pharmaceutical companies.

The acquisition of Ranbaxy was a calculated risk that required careful integration of the two companies' operations, cultures, and product portfolios. Shanghvi's ability to manage this complex process and realize synergies between the two companies demonstrated his strategic thinking and leadership capabilities. This move not only increased Sun Pharma's market presence but also enhanced its R&D capabilities and product offerings.

Focus on Operational Excellence

Shanghvi's leadership has always emphasized operational excellence. He has consistently focused on optimizing processes, reducing costs, and improving efficiency across the company's operations. This approach has enabled Sun Pharmaceuticals to maintain high standards of quality and compliance while achieving significant cost savings.

Shanghvi's attention to detail and commitment to excellence have been key factors in Sun Pharmaceuticals' success. His leadership has fostered a culture of continuous improvement, where employees are encouraged to seek efficiencies and innovations in their work. This focus on operational excellence has positioned Sun Pharma as a leader in the highly competitive pharmaceutical industry.

My Story with a Transformational Leader

These were the examples of renowned leaders from the history of pharmacy and healthcare. But for each one of us, there is a leader/ mentor in our lives. I would like to share with you the story of a person from my life who had a great impact on me as a mentor. He helped me a lot with my confidence in the early years of my career and still continues to be a guiding light in my life.

In the bustling world of pharmaceuticals, where success often hinges on the delicate balance of product knowledge, communication skills, and personal connections, there emerged a figure whose influence would shape not just careers but lives. This is the story of how **Mr. Sunil Munjaral,** an Area Business Manager at Zydus Cadila, became a guiding light in my journey as a medical representative stationed in Sikar.

As a medical representative, navigating the intricacies of pharmaceutical sales was a daily challenge. Yet, it was within these challenges that the seeds of transformation were sown, waiting for the right mentor to nurture them. That mentor arrived in the form of Sunil Munjaral, whose arrival heralded a shift in perspective and approach.

I learned many lessons from Sunil that helped me navigate my journey in the pharmaceutical industry.

Sunil's first lesson was simple yet profound: mastery of one's product is the cornerstone of effective communication. Through his guidance, it became evident that trust in the product was the bedrock upon which fruitful interactions with doctors were built. This wasn't just about pushing pills; it was about genuinely believing in the value they provided to patients.

But Sunil's teachings extended far beyond the realm of sales tactics. He emphasized the importance of empathy and compassion in every interaction. Recognizing doctors not just as prescribers, but as fellow humans with their own hopes, fears, and aspirations was key. Understanding this allowed for a deeper connection, one built on mutual respect and understanding.

"Doctors are human too," Sunil would remind, his words carrying the weight of wisdom. It wasn't about lavish gifts or superficial gestures; it was about fostering genuine relationships grounded in sincerity and care. His analogy of treating doctors like close friends, with daily reminders and gestures of appreciation, underscored the importance of nurturing connections for the long term.

Sunil's advice and guidance helped me a lot with my confidence and professional growth. To all the people in positions out there, I request you all to be the leaders who lead by action. I try to emulate the lessons Sunil taught me till this date because he led by action.

With further chapters in the book, I wish to provide you with more insights into how you can work on your leadership styles and be the healthcare leader that our industry and our country needs.

Chapter 3
Empathy: The Cornerstone of Leadership

Don't you feel an immense sense of happiness and positivity when you are listened and feel understood by your family, friends, colleagues, or sometimes even by strangers? Yes, that's the power of empathy.

Empathy in leadership refers to the ability to understand and share the feelings of others. This includes not only recognizing the emotions and perspectives of employees and stakeholders but also responding to them appropriately. An empathetic leader is someone who actively listens, shows genuine concern, and takes the time to understand the needs and concerns of their team members and other stakeholders. This approach goes beyond mere sympathy, which is feeling compassion or sorrow for others. It involves a deeper connection and an effort to see things from others' viewpoints.

In the context of leadership, empathy facilitates better communication, fosters stronger relationships, and promotes a more supportive and inclusive work environment. It is about creating an atmosphere where employees feel valued and understood. This leads to increased motivation, loyalty, and productivity. Empathetic leaders are often more effective in resolving conflicts. They are able to appreciate the different perspectives involved and work towards solutions that consider everyone's interests.

Importance of Empathy in the Pharmaceutical Industry

In the pharmaceutical industry, empathy is particularly crucial due to its direct impact on human health and well-being. The stakes are high, and decisions made within pharmaceutical companies can profoundly affect patients' lives. Empathetic leadership ensures that patient needs and concerns are always at the forefront of decision-making processes. This patient-centric approach leads to more ethical practices, better patient outcomes, and innovations that truly address the needs of the population.

Empathetic leaders prioritize the well-being of patients, ensuring that the development and distribution of drugs are conducted with the highest ethical standards. By focusing on the human element, they drive the creation of treatments that improve quality of life and address unmet medical needs. This commitment to empathy can also enhance public trust in pharmaceutical companies, fostering a positive reputation and long-term success.

Moreover, the pharmaceutical industry involves a diverse range of stakeholders, including researchers, healthcare professionals, regulators, and patients. Empathetic leaders are better equipped to navigate these complex relationships, fostering collaboration and trust among all parties involved. This is essential for successful drug development, regulatory compliance, and market acceptance. Understanding the perspectives and challenges faced by different stakeholders enables leaders to build stronger partnerships and drive collective success.

Internally, empathy plays a critical role in addressing the challenges within pharmaceutical companies. Pharmaceutical organizations often operate under intense pressure to innovate while adhering to strict regulatory standards. An empathetic leadership style helps mitigate stress, reduce burnout, and enhance overall employee well-being. By understanding and addressing the concerns of their employees, leaders can create a more positive and productive work environment, leading to higher job satisfaction, increased loyalty, and improved performance. Empathy thus serves as a cornerstone for building resilient, innovative, and ethically sound pharmaceutical organizations.

The purpose of this chapter is to explore the concept of empathy in leadership within the context of the Indian pharmaceutical industry. It aims to highlight how empathetic leadership can drive patient-centric innovation, organizational success, and improved stakeholder relationships. This chapter will provide a comprehensive understanding of why empathy is a critical quality for leaders in this sector and how it can be cultivated and implemented effectively.

Empathy and Patient-Centric Innovation

Empathy allows leaders to step into the shoes of patients, gaining insight into their challenges, fears, and aspirations. This understanding is crucial for developing medications and treatments that truly address patient needs rather than merely achieving scientific or commercial milestones. By fostering a culture of empathy, pharmaceutical companies can drive innovations that improve patient outcomes and enhance quality of life.

Empathetic leadership encourages the inclusion of patient perspectives at every stage of the drug development process. This involves soliciting feedback from patients during clinical trials, incorporating their experiences into the design of treatment protocols, and ensuring that end products are user-friendly and accessible. For example, understanding the daily struggles of patients with chronic conditions can lead to the development of medications with fewer side effects, easier administration methods, and better compliance rates.

Examples of Patient-Centric Innovations Driven by Empathetic Leadership

Several innovations in the pharmaceutical industry have been driven by empathetic leadership. For instance, the development of fixed-dose combination (FDC) drugs, which combine multiple medications into a single pill, has significantly improved adherence rates among patients with chronic illnesses such as HIV/AIDS and diabetes. This innovation stemmed from an understanding of the difficulties patients face in managing complex medication regimens.

Another example is the creation of patient support programs that provide comprehensive care beyond just medication. These programs often include educational resources, counseling services, and adherence support, all designed to address the holistic needs of patients. Empathetic leaders recognize that managing a disease is not solely about taking medication but also about coping with the emotional and practical challenges of living with a chronic condition.

Comprehensive Patient Support Programs

Another significant innovation driven by empathetic leadership is the creation of comprehensive patient support programs. These programs go beyond providing medication, offering a range of services designed to address the holistic needs of patients managing chronic conditions.

Holistic Care Approach: Empathetic leaders understand that managing a chronic disease involves more than just taking medication. Patients often face emotional, psychological, and practical challenges that can impact their overall well-being and treatment adherence. Comprehensive patient support programs are designed to provide holistic care, including educational resources, counseling services, and adherence support.

Empathy's Role in Fostering Collaboration and Innovation Within Teams

Empathy is a cornerstone in building a collaborative and innovative culture within any organization, and it is particularly vital in the pharmaceutical sector. This industry relies heavily on the synergy of various departments—such as research and development (R&D), regulatory affairs, and marketing—to successfully bring new drugs to market. Empathetic leaders play a crucial role in facilitating this collaboration by ensuring that all team members feel heard, valued, and respected.

One of the primary ways empathetic leaders foster collaboration is by recognizing and appreciating the unique contributions and perspectives of each team member. In the pharmaceutical industry, where cross-functional teams often include scientists, medical professionals, regulatory experts, and marketing strategists, this inclusivity is essential. By valuing diverse viewpoints, empathetic leaders can break down organizational silos and promote a more integrated approach to problem-solving. This environment encourages team members to share their ideas and suggestions more openly, leading to a richer pool of innovative solutions.

Moreover, empathy helps leaders understand the personal and professional aspirations of their employees. This understanding allows leaders to align these individual goals with the broader objectives of the organization, fostering a sense of purpose and motivation among employees. When employees feel that their personal growth is linked to the success of the company, they are more likely to go above and beyond in their roles. This is especially critical in the pharmaceutical industry, which thrives on continuous innovation to develop groundbreaking treatments and maintain a competitive edge.

Empathetic leadership also plays a vital role in managing the inherent stresses and pressures associated with the pharmaceutical industry. The industry is characterized by high stakes, stringent regulatory standards, and intense competition. Leaders who demonstrate empathy can help mitigate stress and reduce burnout by creating a supportive and understanding work environment. This not only enhances employee well-being but also improves overall productivity and job satisfaction, leading to better organizational outcomes.

Example of Successful Indian Pharmaceutical Companies Emphasizing Empathy

Lupin Pharmaceuticals: Emphasizing Empathy in Leadership

Lupin Pharmaceuticals, a major player in the Indian pharmaceutical industry, has consistently emphasized empathy in its leadership approach. Founded in 1968 by Dr. Desh Bandhu Gupta, Lupin has grown to become one of the largest generic pharmaceutical companies in the world, renowned for its commitment to quality, innovation, and patient care.

Empathy in Leadership: Lupin's leadership has placed a strong emphasis on empathy as a core leadership value. This approach has been instrumental in shaping the company's strategies and operations.

Patient-Centric Initiatives: Lupin's empathetic leadership is evident in its patient-centric initiatives. The company has developed a range of affordable medications for chronic diseases such as tuberculosis, cardiovascular diseases, diabetes, and respiratory conditions. By understanding the financial and emotional burdens faced by patients, Lupin has focused on making essential medications accessible to all, especially in developing regions.

Community Engagement: Lupin's empathetic approach extends to its community engagement efforts. The Lupin Human Welfare & Research Foundation (LHWRF) has been actively involved in improving healthcare access in rural areas. The foundation works on various health initiatives, including free medical camps, health awareness programs, and sanitation projects, addressing the holistic needs of underserved communities.

Lupin Pharmaceuticals exemplifies how empathetic leadership can lead to significant advancements in both patient care and organizational success. By prioritizing empathy in its interactions with patients, communities, and employees, Lupin has set a benchmark in the pharmaceutical industry, demonstrating that compassionate leadership is key to sustainable growth and positive societal impact.

Empathy and Stakeholder Relationships

Empathy plays a crucial role in building and maintaining strong relationships with various stakeholders in the pharmaceutical industry, including patients, healthcare providers, and regulators. These relationships are essential for the success of pharmaceutical companies, as they directly impact patient outcomes, regulatory compliance, and overall business sustainability.

Building Trust with Patients

In the pharmaceutical industry, patient trust is paramount. Patients rely on pharmaceutical companies to provide safe and effective treatments that improve their health and well-being. Empathetic leaders understand the fears, concerns, and needs of patients, which allows them to develop medications and treatment options that prioritize patient safety and comfort.

Empathy in this context involves actively listening to patient feedback, understanding their experiences with medications, and addressing their concerns. For example, an empathetic approach might involve patient advisory boards, where patients can provide direct input into the development and marketing of new medications. This not only helps companies develop products that better meet patient needs but also builds trust and loyalty among patients who feel their voices are heard and valued.

Building Trust with Healthcare Providers

Healthcare providers, including doctors, nurses, and pharmacists, are critical stakeholders in the pharmaceutical industry. Empathetic leadership involves understanding the challenges and pressures faced by healthcare providers and supporting them in providing optimal patient care. This might include providing educational resources, clinical trial support, and continuing medical education opportunities.

For example, empathetic leaders might collaborate with healthcare providers to develop educational programs that help them better understand new medications or treatment protocols. By demonstrating a commitment to improving patient outcomes and supporting healthcare providers in their daily practice, pharmaceutical companies can build strong, collaborative relationships with the healthcare community.

Building Trust with Regulators

Regulatory bodies play a crucial role in ensuring the safety, efficacy, and quality of pharmaceutical products. Empathetic leaders recognize the challenges and pressures faced by regulators and work to build transparent and cooperative relationships. This might involve proactive communication, adherence to regulatory guidelines, and a commitment to continuous improvement in quality and safety standards.

For example, empathetic leaders engage with regulators early in the drug development process to address potential concerns and ensure compliance with regulatory requirements. By demonstrating a commitment to patient safety and regulatory compliance, pharmaceutical companies can build trust with regulators and streamline the approval process for new medications.

The Impact of Empathy on Customer Satisfaction and Loyalty

Empathy has a profound impact on customer satisfaction and loyalty in the pharmaceutical industry. Patients and healthcare providers are more likely to trust and remain loyal to companies that demonstrate empathy in their interactions and decision-making processes.

Customer Satisfaction

Empathetic leaders focus on understanding and meeting the needs of their customers, which can lead to higher levels of customer satisfaction. For patients, this might mean developing medications that are easy to use, have minimal side effects, and improve quality of life. For healthcare providers, this might mean providing educational resources, clinical support, and responsive customer service.

For example, pharmaceutical companies that invest in patient support programs or offer financial assistance to patients who cannot afford their medications demonstrate empathy and can significantly enhance customer satisfaction.

Customer Loyalty

Empathy also plays a crucial role in building customer loyalty. Patients and healthcare providers are more likely to remain loyal to companies that prioritize their needs and well-being. This loyalty can translate into repeat business, positive word-of-mouth recommendations, and long-term partnerships.

For instance, pharmaceutical companies that engage with patient advocacy groups, participate in community health initiatives, and provide ongoing support to healthcare providers are perceived as empathetic and caring organizations. This positive reputation can strengthen customer loyalty and differentiate the company from its competitors.

Strategies for Fostering an Empathetic Culture

Empathy is not just a trait but a skill that can be cultivated and developed within an organization, particularly in the pharmaceutical industry where patient-centricity and stakeholder relationships are paramount. Fostering an empathetic culture requires deliberate strategies and initiatives aimed at leadership training and development, as well as organizational practices that prioritize empathy in decision-making and interactions.

Leadership Training and Development

Leadership training and development programs are essential for fostering an empathetic culture within pharmaceutical companies. These programs aim to enhance the empathy skills of leaders, empowering them to understand and respond effectively to the needs and concerns of their teams, patients, and other stakeholders.

1. **Empathy Workshops and Seminars:**

Empathy workshops and seminars provide leaders with opportunities to learn about the importance of empathy in leadership and its practical applications. These sessions often include interactive exercises, role-playing, and case studies to help leaders develop a deeper understanding of empathy and its impact on organizational success.

For example, a workshop might involve scenarios where leaders practice active listening and responding empathetically to team members' concerns or patient feedback. Role-playing exercises can simulate difficult conversations with patients or healthcare providers to help leaders develop skills in empathy-driven communication.

2. **Leadership Coaching:**
Leadership coaching is another effective method for developing empathy skills among leaders. Coaches work one-on-one with leaders to help them identify their strengths and areas for improvement in empathy. Coaches provide feedback, guidance, and support to help leaders enhance their emotional intelligence and empathy capabilities.

Coaches may use tools such as empathy assessments or 360-degree feedback to help leaders gain insights into their empathy levels and how their behavior impacts others. This personalized approach allows leaders to develop empathy in a way that is tailored to their unique leadership style and organizational context.

3. **Role Modeling by Senior Leaders:**

Senior leaders play a crucial role in shaping organizational culture through their behavior and actions. By demonstrating empathy in their own interactions and decision-making processes, senior leaders set an example for others to follow. This can include making time to listen to employees' concerns, showing appreciation for their contributions, and advocating for patient-centered practices.

For instance, a senior leader might prioritize attending patient advisory board meetings or participating in patient support programs to understand patient needs firsthand. By visibly demonstrating empathy, senior leaders create a culture where empathy is valued and expected at all levels of the organization.

Benefits of Leadership Training and Development in Empathy

1. **Enhanced Employee Engagement:**

   Leadership training in empathy can lead to higher levels of employee engagement and satisfaction. When employees feel that their leaders understand and care about their concerns, they are more likely to be motivated and committed to their work. This can result in improved productivity, lower turnover rates, and a positive work environment.

2. **Improved Patient Outcomes:**
   Empathetic leadership has a direct impact on patient outcomes. Leaders who prioritize empathy are better able to understand patient needs and concerns, leading to the development of medications and treatment protocols that are more effective and patient-friendly. This can result in better adherence to treatment plans, reduced hospital readmissions, and overall improved patient satisfaction.

3. **Stronger Stakeholder Relationships:**

   Leadership development in empathy helps pharmaceutical companies build stronger relationships with stakeholders such as healthcare providers, patients, and regulatory bodies. When leaders demonstrate empathy in their interactions, they build trust and credibility, which is essential for successful collaborations and partnerships.

Leadership training and development programs are critical for fostering an empathetic culture within pharmaceutical companies. By investing in empathy skills, leaders can create a workplace environment where empathy is valued and practiced, leading to enhanced employee engagement, improved patient outcomes, and stronger stakeholder relationships. Empathy-driven leadership not only drives organizational success but also ensures that pharmaceutical companies are better positioned to meet the diverse needs of their stakeholders in an increasingly complex healthcare landscape.

Creating an Empathetic Work Environment

Creating an empathetic work environment in the pharmaceutical industry is crucial for fostering collaboration, innovation, and employee well-being. Pharmaceutical companies operate in a high-stakes environment where patient outcomes and regulatory compliance are paramount. Empathy among staff, particularly in leadership roles, can significantly impact organizational success and patient care. This section explores policies, practices, and the importance of open communication and active listening in creating an empathetic work environment.

Policies and Practices that Promote Empathy Among Staff

1. **Leadership Commitment:**

   Leadership plays a pivotal role in promoting empathy within an organization. Senior leaders should lead by example, demonstrating empathy in their interactions with employees, patients, and other stakeholders. This commitment to empathy should be reflected in the organization's mission, vision, and values.

2. **Clear Communication Channels:**

   Establishing clear and open communication channels is essential for promoting empathy. Employees should feel comfortable sharing their thoughts, concerns, and feedback with their supervisors and colleagues. This can be facilitated through regular team meetings, one-on-one sessions, and anonymous feedback mechanisms.

3. **Employee Assistance Programs (EAPs):**

   EAPs can provide employees with access to counseling services, stress management techniques, and resources for dealing with personal and professional challenges. These programs demonstrate the organization's commitment to supporting employees' well-being and mental health, fostering a culture of empathy and care.

4. **Recognition and Appreciation:**

   Recognizing and appreciating employees' contributions can boost morale and create a positive work environment. Leaders should acknowledge employees' efforts and achievements, demonstrating empathy and understanding of their hard work and dedication.

5. **Flexibility and Work-Life Balance:**

   Offering flexible work arrangements and promoting work-life balance can show empathy toward employees' personal needs and responsibilities. This can include options for remote work, flexible hours, and parental leave policies that support employees in achieving a healthy balance between work and personal life.

Importance of Open Communication and Active Listening

1. **Building Trust:**

   Open communication and active listening build trust between leaders and employees. When employees feel heard and valued, they are more likely to be engaged and committed to their work. This trust is essential for fostering a collaborative and supportive work environment.

2. **Empowering Employees:**

   Active listening empowers employees by giving them a voice in decision-making processes. When leaders actively listen to their concerns and ideas, they demonstrate respect and empathy, which encourages employees to contribute to the organization's success.

3. **Conflict Resolution:**

   Open communication and active listening are critical for resolving conflicts effectively. When disagreements arise, leaders who practice empathy can mediate conflicts and find solutions that satisfy all parties involved. This reduces tension and improves team dynamics.

4. **Enhancing Innovation:**

   Open communication encourages the sharing of ideas and perspectives, which can lead to innovative solutions. Employees who feel comfortable expressing their thoughts and opinions are more likely to contribute new ideas that can benefit the organization and its stakeholders.

5. **Improving Patient Care:**

   In the pharmaceutical industry, open communication and active listening are essential for understanding patient needs and concerns. By listening to patients, healthcare providers, and regulators, pharmaceutical companies can develop medications and treatments that meet the highest standards of safety, efficacy, and patient satisfaction.

Empathy in Decision-Making

Incorporating empathy into corporate governance and decision-making processes is crucial for pharmaceutical companies, as it directly impacts patient outcomes, employee satisfaction, and stakeholder relationships. Let us explore the significance of empathy in decision-making and gain insights into how pharmaceutical companies can integrate empathetic practices into their corporate governance.

Incorporating Empathy into Corporate Governance

1. **Ethical Frameworks and Guidelines:**

   Developing and implementing ethical frameworks and guidelines ensures that decisions are aligned with the organization's values and principles, including empathy.

   Example: Johnson & Johnson's Credo guides decision-making by emphasizing responsibility to patients, employees, communities, and shareholders, fostering an empathetic corporate culture.

2. **Stakeholder Engagement:**
   Engaging with stakeholders, including patients, healthcare providers, and community representatives, provides insights into their needs and preferences, informing empathetic

decision-making.

Example: GlaxoSmithKline holds regular stakeholder meetings and advisory panels to gather feedback on decision-making processes, ensuring that decisions reflect empathy and respect for stakeholder perspectives.

3. **Measuring Impact:**

   Implementing metrics to measure the impact of decisions on patients, employees, and stakeholders ensures accountability and transparency in empathetic decision-making.

   Example: Merck & Co. conducts patient satisfaction surveys and employee engagement surveys to evaluate the impact of decisions on stakeholders, using feedback to refine decision-making processes.

Enhancing Staff Relations Through Empathy

Empathy plays a crucial role in building stronger teams and improving morale within pharmaceutical companies. In an industry that operates under intense pressure to innovate and adhere to strict regulatory standards, fostering a culture of empathy can significantly enhance staff relations and overall organizational effectiveness.

Building Stronger Teams

1. **Creating a Supportive Environment:**

   Empathetic leaders create a supportive environment where team members feel valued, respected, and understood. This is particularly important in the pharmaceutical industry, where teams are often multidisciplinary, consisting of researchers, clinicians, regulatory experts, and marketers. Each team member brings unique perspectives and expertise, and empathy helps leaders appreciate and leverage these differences.

For example, leaders can organize team-building activities that promote understanding and collaboration among team members. These activities may include team lunches, offsite meetings, or workshops focused on improving communication and teamwork.

2. **Improving Communication:**

   Empathy improves communication within teams by encouraging open dialogue and active listening. Leaders who practice empathy are better able to understand their team members' perspectives, concerns, and ideas. This leads to more effective problem-solving and decision-making processes, as team members feel comfortable sharing their thoughts and suggestions.

   Techniques such as active listening, paraphrasing, and asking open-ended questions can enhance communication within teams. Leaders can also encourage regular team meetings or check-ins to provide opportunities for team members to share updates, ask questions, and address any challenges they may be facing.

Techniques for Fostering Empathy Within Teams

1. **Training and Development:**

   Providing training and development opportunities focused on empathy can help team members understand its importance and develop their empathy skills. Workshops, seminars, and webinars on empathy, emotional intelligence, and communication can provide team members with practical tools and techniques for fostering empathy in their daily interactions.

For instance, leaders can conduct empathy workshops where team members engage in role-playing exercises to practice empathetic communication and problem-solving. These exercises can simulate real-life scenarios that team members may encounter in their roles, such as dealing with patient concerns or navigating interdepartmental conflicts.

2. **Encouraging Empathetic Behaviors:**

   Leaders can encourage empathetic behaviors within teams by recognizing and rewarding acts of empathy. This can include publicly acknowledging team members who demonstrate empathy in their interactions with colleagues, patients, or other stakeholders.

   For example, leaders can implement a peer recognition program where team members nominate each other for demonstrating empathy or supporting their colleagues during challenging times. Recognizing empathetic behaviors reinforces their importance and encourages other team members to follow suit.

3. **Promoting Psychological Safety:**

   Creating a psychologically safe environment is essential for fostering empathy within teams. Psychological safety encourages team members to speak up, share their ideas, and take risks without fear of judgment or reprisal. Leaders can promote psychological safety by demonstrating vulnerability, encouraging diverse perspectives, and valuing constructive feedback.

   For instance, leaders can use team meetings to discuss failures or setbacks openly and encourage team members to share their thoughts on how to improve. This transparency helps build trust and encourages empathy, as team members feel supported in taking risks and learning from their experiences.

Empathy plays a pivotal role in enhancing staff relations within pharmaceutical companies by building stronger teams, improving morale, and fostering a collaborative work environment. Leaders who prioritize empathy create a culture where team members feel valued and supported, leading to improved communication, increased engagement, and ultimately, better organizational performance. By investing in empathy, pharmaceutical companies can cultivate a workplace culture that drives innovation, improves patient outcomes, and sustains long-term success.

Addressing Conflict and Fostering Inclusion with Empathy

Conflict is inevitable in any workplace, including the pharmaceutical industry, which operates under high stakes and pressure. However, how conflicts are managed can significantly impact team morale, productivity, and ultimately, the success of the organization. Empathy plays a crucial role in resolving conflicts constructively and creating an inclusive workplace where every team member feels valued and respected.

Strategies for Using Empathy to Resolve Conflicts

1. **Understanding Perspectives:**

   Empathetic leaders approach conflicts by first seeking to understand the perspectives and emotions of all parties involved. This involves active listening, putting oneself in the other person's shoes, and acknowledging their feelings and concerns. By understanding the underlying reasons for conflict, leaders can address the root causes more effectively. For example, if there is a conflict between research and regulatory teams regarding the timeline for a new drug approval, an empathetic leader would listen to both sides, acknowledge their concerns, and work towards a solution that meets both scientific and regulatory requirements.

2. **Promoting Open Communication:**

   Empathy encourages open and honest communication among team members, which is essential for resolving conflicts. Leaders can create a safe space where team members feel comfortable expressing their thoughts, concerns, and emotions without fear of judgment.

   Techniques such as active listening, paraphrasing, and asking clarifying questions can facilitate effective communication. Leaders can also encourage team members to use "I" statements to express their feelings and perspectives, which fosters empathy and mutual understanding.

3. **Finding Common Ground:**

   Empathetic leaders look for areas of common ground and shared interests among conflicting parties. This helps in finding solutions that benefit both sides and promote collaboration rather than competition.

   For instance, in a conflict between marketing and research teams over the launch strategy of a new drug, an empathetic leader might identify the shared goal of patient access and develop a compromise that satisfies both teams' concerns.

4. **Encouraging Collaboration:**

   Collaboration is key to resolving conflicts and fostering a sense of unity within teams. Empathetic leaders encourage collaboration by bringing conflicting parties together to work towards a common goal.

   Team-building activities, joint problem-solving sessions, and cross-functional projects can help build trust and understanding among team members. These activities promote empathy by allowing team members to see each other's strengths, perspectives, and challenges.

5. **Mediating Conflicts Fairly:**

   When conflicts arise, empathetic leaders act as mediators to facilitate constructive dialogue and negotiation. They remain impartial and fair, ensuring that all parties have an opportunity to express their views and participate in finding a resolution. Mediation involves active listening, reframing issues, and helping parties to explore creative solutions. This process promotes empathy by demonstrating respect for all perspectives and fostering a collaborative approach to conflict resolution.

Strategies for Creating an Inclusive Workplace

1. **Promoting Diversity and Inclusion:**

   Empathetic leaders prioritize diversity and inclusion within their teams and organizations. They recognize the value of diverse perspectives and backgrounds in driving innovation and problem-solving.

   Leaders can promote diversity by implementing inclusive hiring practices, supporting employee resource groups, and fostering a culture of respect and acceptance. This creates a workplace where all team members feel valued for their unique contributions.

2. **Empowering Underrepresented Voices:**

   Empathy involves recognizing and addressing the needs of underrepresented groups within the organization. Leaders can empower underrepresented voices by providing opportunities for career development, mentorship, and leadership roles. For example, leaders can establish mentoring programs where senior executives mentor employees from underrepresented groups to help them advance in their careers. This promotes empathy by demonstrating a commitment to supporting the growth and success of all team members.

3. **Creating a Safe and Respectful Environment:** An inclusive workplace is built on a foundation of psychological safety, where team members feel safe to express their opinions, ask questions, and challenge the status quo without fear of retaliation.

   Leaders can create a safe environment by addressing bias and discrimination, promoting open communication, and enforcing policies that uphold respect and fairness. This fosters empathy by ensuring that all team members feel valued and respected for who they are.

4. **Training and Development:**

   Providing training and development opportunities on diversity, inclusion, and unconscious bias can help team members and leaders enhance their empathy skills. Workshops, seminars, and online courses can provide practical tools and techniques for fostering empathy and creating an inclusive workplace culture. These programs promote empathy by increasing awareness of diverse perspectives and encouraging empathy-driven behaviors.

Empathy stands as a cornerstone of effective leadership, particularly within the complex and impactful realm of the pharmaceutical industry. As discussed throughout this chapter, empathetic leadership plays a critical role in driving organizational success, fostering collaboration, and creating an inclusive workplace culture.

Empathy is not just a soft skill; it's a fundamental aspect of effective leadership in the pharmaceutical industry. As leaders, we must embrace and prioritize empathy in our interactions with patients, employees, and stakeholders. By doing so, we can create a more compassionate, innovative, and sustainable healthcare ecosystem.

Empathetic leadership is not without its challenges, but the rewards—enhanced patient outcomes, improved employee engagement, and a positive organizational culture—are well worth the effort. Therefore, I encourage all leaders in the pharmaceutical industry to:

- **Invest in Leadership Development:** Commit to developing empathy skills through training and coaching programs for current and aspiring leaders.
- **Promote Inclusivity:** Create a workplace where diverse perspectives are valued, and all team members feel respected and heard.
- **Lead by Example:** Demonstrate empathy in your daily interactions and decision-making processes, inspiring others to do the same.
- **Monitor Progress:** Regularly assess and evaluate the effectiveness of empathy-building initiatives and adjust strategies as needed.

By embracing empathy, we can not only drive organizational success but also make a positive impact on the lives of patients and communities we serve. Together, let's build a future where empathetic leadership is the norm in the pharmaceutical industry.

In conclusion, empathy is not just a leadership trait; it's a transformative force that can shape the future of healthcare. Let's lead with empathy, lead with heart, and create a more compassionate and innovative pharmaceutical industry.

Chapter 4
Innovative Solutions Through Empathy

In the previous chapter, we discussed how empathy is an essential cornerstone of leadership in the pharmaceutical industry.

Empathy-driven innovation is a transformative approach in the pharmaceutical industry that prioritizes understanding and addressing the needs of patients. In the context of India's unique healthcare landscape, the importance of empathy cannot be overstated. India faces numerous healthcare challenges, including a high burden of diseases, limited access to healthcare services, and significant disparities in health outcomes across different regions and socioeconomic groups.

These challenges are compounded by the diverse and often complex healthcare needs of India's vast population. Empathy-driven innovation is essential in addressing these issues effectively. By genuinely understanding the struggles and concerns of patients, especially those from marginalized communities, pharmaceutical companies can create solutions that are not only medically effective but also accessible and affordable as we have emphasized in previous chapters as well.

The purpose of this chapter is to explore how empathy fosters innovation in addressing healthcare challenges unique to India. It aims to highlight the critical role of empathy in driving patient-centric innovations that can transform healthcare outcomes. The chapter will delve into the concept of empathy-driven innovation, provide an overview of the unique healthcare challenges in India, and present case studies showcasing successful empathy-driven initiatives by Indian pharmaceutical companies. Additionally, it will offer strategies for fostering an empathetic culture within organizations and discuss the challenges and opportunities associated with empathy-driven innovation. Through this exploration, the chapter seeks to inspire leaders in the pharmaceutical industry to prioritize empathy in their innovation efforts.

Understanding Empathy-Driven Innovation

Empathy-driven innovation in healthcare and pharmaceuticals refers to the practice of designing and developing products, services, and solutions that are deeply informed by the lived experiences, needs, and challenges of patients and other stakeholders.

This approach requires companies to go beyond traditional metrics of success and efficiency, and instead prioritize understanding and addressing the holistic needs of patients.

In the pharmaceutical industry, empathy-driven innovation might involve creating medications that are not only effective but also easier to take, developing patient support programs that address emotional and practical challenges, and ensuring that new technologies are accessible to diverse populations. This form of innovation is rooted in human-centered design principles, which emphasize empathy and a thorough understanding of users' perspectives throughout the development process.

The Importance of Empathy in Healthcare

Empathy is crucial in healthcare for several reasons:

1. **Understanding Patient Needs**: Empathy allows healthcare providers and pharmaceutical companies to gain a deeper understanding of patients' experiences, fears, and daily challenges. This understanding is essential for developing treatments and interventions that are truly effective. For example, an empathetic approach can reveal that patients struggle with complex medication regimens, leading to the development of simpler, more manageable treatment plans.

2. **Improving Patient Outcomes**: When pharmaceutical companies prioritize empathy, they are better equipped to create products that patients are more likely to use correctly and consistently.

   This adherence to treatment protocols can significantly improve health outcomes. For instance, creating user-friendly medication packaging or providing comprehensive patient education can enhance adherence and effectiveness.

3. **Fostering Trust and Engagement**: Empathy-driven practices help build trust between patients and healthcare providers. When patients feel understood and valued, they are more likely to engage actively in their treatment plans and communicate openly with their healthcare providers. This trust is crucial for gathering accurate patient data, which in turn informs more effective treatment strategies.

4. **Addressing Disparities in Healthcare**: Empathy-driven innovation is particularly important in addressing healthcare disparities. By understanding the unique needs of different patient populations, pharmaceutical companies can develop solutions that are accessible and equitable. This might involve designing affordable medication options or creating programs that support underserved communities.

5. **Driving Ethical Practices**: Empathy ensures that ethical considerations are at the forefront of pharmaceutical innovation.

   When companies prioritize the well-being of patients, they are more likely to engage in practices that promote transparency, fairness, and social responsibility. This ethical grounding is essential for maintaining public trust and ensuring the long-term sustainability of the industry.

Connection Between Empathy and Innovation

Empathy is a catalyst for creativity and innovation in the pharmaceutical industry because it enables a deep understanding of the needs and experiences of patients, healthcare providers, and other stakeholders. This understanding is critical for identifying gaps in existing treatments and developing novel solutions that address these gaps effectively.

1. **Identifying Unmet Needs**: Empathy allows pharmaceutical companies to see beyond clinical data and statistics. By engaging with patients and listening to their stories, companies can identify unmet needs that may not be evident through traditional research methods. For instance, understanding the daily struggles of patients with chronic illnesses can lead to the development of more user-friendly medication delivery systems, such as patches or inhalers instead of pills.

2. **Enhancing User Experience**: Empathetic insights can drive the design of products and services that improve the overall user experience. For example, by empathizing with patients who have difficulty adhering to complex medication regimens, companies can innovate by creating combination drugs that simplify treatment protocols, thereby improving adherence and outcomes.

3. **Fostering Collaboration**: Empathy fosters a collaborative environment within pharmaceutical companies by encouraging open communication and teamwork. When leaders and employees understand and appreciate each other's perspectives, they are more likely to work together effectively, share ideas, and innovate. This collaborative spirit is essential for brainstorming and developing breakthrough solutions.

4. **Driving Ethical Innovation**: Empathetic leaders are more likely to consider the ethical implications of their innovations. This can lead to the development of treatments that are not only effective but also affordable and accessible to a broader population. For instance, an empathetic approach might drive a company to focus on developing low-cost medications for diseases prevalent in low-income regions.

5. **Encouraging Patient-Centered Research**: Empathy shifts the focus of research and development towards patient-centered outcomes.

   This means that clinical trials and studies are designed with the patient's experience in mind, leading to innovations that truly enhance quality of life. For example, understanding the side effects that patients find most troubling can lead to the development of drugs with fewer or more tolerable side effects.

The Unique Healthcare Challenges in India

India faces significant healthcare challenges due to its vast and diverse population. Major issues include a high disease burden from both communicable and non-communicable diseases, These challenges have profound impacts on the population,

Need for Innovative Solutions

The unique healthcare challenges in India necessitate the development and implementation of empathetic, innovative solutions to effectively address the diverse and complex needs of the population. Traditional approaches often fall short in tackling issues Thus, innovative strategies driven by empathy are crucial for creating sustainable improvements in health outcomes.

Empathetic Understanding: Empathy enables healthcare leaders and innovators to gain a deeper understanding of the real-world problems faced by patients and communities. By putting themselves in the shoes of patients, leaders can design solutions that are not only effective but also tailored to the specific needs and circumstances of those they aim to serve.

This patient-centric approach ensures that innovations are practical, acceptable, and impactful.

Collaborative Efforts: Empathetic innovation fosters collaboration among various stakeholders, including healthcare providers, patients, researchers, and policymakers. This collaborative approach ensures that solutions are multifaceted and leverage the strengths and insights of all parties involved. It encourages shared responsibility and collective action towards common health goals.

Addressing Socioeconomic Barriers: Empathy-driven solutions are sensitive to the socioeconomic barriers that hinder access to healthcare. By considering factors such as affordability and literacy, these innovations ensure that even the most disadvantaged populations can benefit. Initiatives like affordable generic medications and community health education programs are prime examples of how empathy can drive equitable healthcare solutions.

The need for empathetic, innovative solutions in India's healthcare sector is paramount. Such solutions not only address the immediate healthcare challenges but also contribute to long-term, sustainable improvements in public health. By focusing on the needs and experiences of patients, empathetic innovation can transform the healthcare landscape, ensuring that every individual has access to the care they need.

Case Study of Empathy-Driven Initiatives in Indian Pharma

Glenmark Pharmaceuticals

Initiative: Comprehensive Patient Support Programs

Introduction to Glenmark's Patient Support Programs Glenmark Pharmaceuticals, a prominent player in the Indian pharmaceutical industry, has demonstrated a deep commitment to patient-centric care through its comprehensive patient support programs. These initiatives are designed to provide holistic support to patients, addressing not just their medical needs but also their educational, emotional, and practical concerns. By integrating empathy into their approach, Glenmark has significantly enhanced patient outcomes and overall well-being.

Components of the Patient Support Programs Glenmark's patient support programs are multifaceted, focusing on several key areas to ensure comprehensive care:

1. **Educational Resources**: Glenmark provides patients with detailed information about their conditions, treatment options, and management strategies. This includes brochures, websites, and mobile apps designed to increase health literacy and empower patients to take control of their health.

2. **Counseling Services**: Recognizing the psychological impact of chronic illnesses, Glenmark offers counseling services to help patients cope with the emotional challenges of their conditions. Trained counselors provide one-on-one support, helping patients manage stress, anxiety, and depression associated with their diagnoses.

3. **Adherence Support**: Medication adherence is a critical factor in the successful management of chronic diseases. Glenmark's programs include reminders, follow-ups, and personalized coaching to ensure patients adhere to their prescribed treatment regimens. This support is crucial in preventing complications and improving long-term health outcomes.

4. **Financial Assistance**: To alleviate the economic burden of chronic illness, Glenmark offers financial assistance programs that help patients afford their medications. This initiative is particularly important in a country where out-of-pocket healthcare expenses can be prohibitive for many families.

Empathy in Addressing Holistic Needs Glenmark's approach to patient support is deeply rooted in empathy, recognizing that effective healthcare extends beyond the mere provision of medications. By understanding and addressing the holistic needs of patients, Glenmark ensures that its support programs are truly patient-centric.

1. **Personalized Care**: Empathy drives Glenmark's commitment to personalized care. By tailoring support to the individual needs of each patient, the company ensures that every patient receives the specific help they require. This personalized approach fosters trust and builds stronger patient-provider relationships.

2. **Emotional Well-being**: Glenmark's emphasis on counseling services underscores the importance of emotional well-being in overall health. Empathetic leaders at Glenmark understand that managing a chronic illness can be an isolating and stressful experience. By providing emotional support, they help patients navigate these challenges more effectively.

3. **Community Engagement**: Glenmark engages with patient communities to better understand their needs and concerns. This engagement is driven by a genuine desire to improve patient lives, reflecting the company's empathetic ethos. By listening to patient voices, Glenmark can continually refine and improve its support programs.

4. **Collaborative Approach**: Empathy fosters collaboration within Glenmark's patient support programs. The company works closely with healthcare providers, caregivers, and patient advocacy groups to create a comprehensive support network. This collaborative approach ensures that patients receive well-rounded care that addresses all aspects of their health.

Impact of the Programs The impact of Glenmark's patient support programs is evident in the improved health outcomes and enhanced quality of life for patients. By addressing educational, emotional, and practical needs, these programs help patients manage their conditions more effectively and confidently. Patients report higher satisfaction levels, better adherence to treatment regimens, and improved overall health.

Glenmark Pharmaceuticals exemplifies how empathy can drive innovation and improve patient care in the pharmaceutical industry. Their comprehensive patient support programs, grounded in empathy, demonstrate a commitment to holistic patient well-being. By focusing on the full spectrum of patient needs—educational, emotional, and practical—Glenmark has set a benchmark for patient-centric care in the industry. This case study highlights the transformative power of empathy in creating effective and compassionate healthcare solutions.

Strategies for Fostering Empathy-Driven Innovation

1. Cultivating Empathy in Leadership

To foster empathy-driven innovation, it is crucial for leaders to cultivate empathy as a core competency within their organizations. Leaders can achieve this by actively listening to their employees, patients, and other stakeholders, ensuring that they understand and address their concerns and needs. This requires leaders to be approachable and open to feedback, creating an environment where team members feel valued and heard.

As discussed in Chapter 3, organizations can implement training and development programs focused on building emotional intelligence and empathetic skills among leaders. Workshops, seminars, and coaching sessions can help leaders enhance their ability to empathize with others. Role-playing scenarios and real-life case studies can be particularly effective in developing these skills, allowing leaders to practice empathy in a controlled setting before applying it in real-world situations.

Leaders should also institutionalize empathy by embedding it into the organization's policies and practices. This can include establishing patient advisory councils to provide direct feedback on healthcare services, creating employee wellness programs that prioritize mental and emotional well-being, and promoting a culture of inclusivity and respect.

By consistently demonstrating empathy in their actions and decisions, leaders can inspire their teams to adopt a similar approach, leading to a more compassionate and innovative organizational culture.

2. Encouraging Patient Interaction

Direct Patient Engagement

One of the most effective ways to foster empathy within pharmaceutical companies is through direct patient interaction. When employees and leaders have the opportunity to meet and interact with patients, they gain firsthand insight into the challenges and experiences these individuals face.

This direct engagement can occur through various means, such as patient focus groups, interviews, and patient advisory panels. By listening to patients' stories and understanding their needs, pharmaceutical professionals can develop a deeper sense of empathy, which is essential for creating patient-centric solutions.

Site Visits and Community Involvement

Organizing site visits to healthcare facilities, community centers, and patient homes can also enhance empathy. These visits allow employees to witness the real-world impact of their products and services, providing a tangible connection between their work and patient outcomes.

Involvement in community health initiatives, such as health camps or disease awareness programs, further reinforces this connection and encourages employees to consider the broader societal implications of their work.

Patient Testimonials and Feedback

Incorporating patient testimonials and feedback into regular company meetings and training sessions can serve as a constant reminder of the importance of empathy. Hearing directly from patients about how medications or treatments have improved their lives—or about the challenges they still face—can be a powerful motivator for innovation. This feedback loop ensures that the patient perspective is always at the forefront of decision-making processes, driving the development of solutions that truly address patient needs.

3. Creating an Empathetic Organizational Culture

Embedding Empathy in Mission and Values

To create an empathetic organizational culture, companies need to embed empathy into their core mission, vision, and values. This means explicitly stating a commitment to understanding and addressing the needs of patients, employees, and other stakeholders. By articulating empathy as a fundamental principle, organizations can set clear expectations for behavior and decision-making at all levels.

Leadership Role Modeling

Leaders play a crucial role in fostering an empathetic culture.

When leaders consistently demonstrate empathy in their interactions and decisions, they set a powerful example for others to follow. This can involve simple acts, such as showing genuine concern for employees' well-being, acknowledging their contributions, and providing support during challenging times. By embodying empathy, leaders can inspire their teams to adopt a similar approach.

Recognition and Rewards

Recognizing and rewarding empathetic behavior can reinforce its importance within the organization. This can involve acknowledging employees who go above and beyond to understand and support patients or colleagues. Establishing awards or incentives for empathetic actions can encourage others to prioritize empathy in their work.

Inclusive Policies and Practices

Creating an inclusive workplace where everyone feels valued and respected is another critical aspect of fostering empathy. This includes implementing policies that promote diversity and inclusion, such as equitable hiring practices, flexible work arrangements, and support for work-life balance. Encouraging open dialogue about diversity and inclusion can also help employees understand and appreciate different perspectives, further embedding empathy into the organizational culture.

Continuous Improvement

Finally, fostering an empathetic culture requires a commitment to continuous improvement. Regularly soliciting feedback from employees, patients, and other stakeholders can help identify areas for enhancement.

Organizations should be willing to adapt and evolve their practices based on this feedback, ensuring that empathy remains a central focus as they grow and change.

By encouraging patient interaction and creating an empathetic organizational culture, pharmaceutical companies can drive innovation and develop solutions that genuinely meet the needs of patients. This approach not only leads to better patient outcomes but also fosters a more engaged and motivated workforce, ultimately contributing to the long-term success of the organization.

Challenges and Opportunities in Empathy-Driven Innovation

Empathy-driven innovation holds significant promise for addressing healthcare challenges in the pharmaceutical industry, but it also presents various challenges and opportunities that must be navigated.

Potential Challenges

Resource Constraints:

One of the primary challenges in implementing empathy-driven initiatives is resource constraints.

Pharmaceutical companies often face budget limitations and competing priorities, which can make it difficult to allocate resources for patient-centric initiatives.

Developing comprehensive patient support programs, conducting patient engagement activities, and embedding empathy into organizational culture requires dedicated financial and human resources. Without adequate investment, these initiatives may not achieve their full potential in improving patient outcomes.

Resistance to Change:

Resistance to change within organizations can also hinder the adoption of empathy-driven innovation. Pharmaceutical companies may have established processes and a culture that prioritizes scientific advancements and regulatory compliance over patient-centered care. Shifting towards an empathetic approach requires a cultural shift and a willingness to embrace new ways of thinking and operating. This can be challenging, especially in large organizations with deeply ingrained practices.

Regulatory and Compliance Considerations:

Navigating regulatory requirements while maintaining an empathetic approach can present challenges. Pharmaceutical companies must adhere to stringent regulations and guidelines to ensure the safety and efficacy of their products. Balancing these requirements with patient needs and preferences requires careful consideration and may necessitate innovative approaches to compliance.

Opportunities for Growth

Improving Patient Outcomes:

Empathy-driven innovation presents a significant opportunity to improve patient outcomes. By understanding patient needs and experiences, pharmaceutical companies can develop medications and treatments that are more effective, safer, and better tolerated. Patient-centric solutions are more likely to enhance medication adherence and reduce the burden of disease, ultimately leading to better health outcomes.

Enhancing Customer Loyalty:

Empathy-driven initiatives can also strengthen customer loyalty and trust. Patients and healthcare providers are more likely to support companies that demonstrate a commitment to understanding and addressing patient needs. Building strong relationships with stakeholders can lead to increased brand reputation, market share, and long-term sustainability.

Driving Innovation and Differentiation:
Empathy fosters creativity and innovation by encouraging pharmaceutical companies to think outside the box. By engaging with patients and understanding their experiences, companies can identify unmet needs and develop novel solutions. This approach can differentiate companies in a competitive market and lead to the

development of breakthrough therapies that address significant health challenges.

Employee Engagement and Satisfaction:

Cultivating an empathetic culture can also enhance employee engagement and satisfaction. When employees feel valued and connected to the mission of improving patient outcomes, they are more motivated and productive. Empathetic leaders who prioritize employee well-being and professional development create a positive work environment that attracts and retains top talent.

Future Outlook

The future of Indian pharma innovation increasingly hinges on the integration of empathy into all facets of the industry. As healthcare systems evolve and patient expectations grow, there is a growing recognition of the importance of patient-centered care. Pharmaceutical companies that embrace empathy-driven innovation will be well-positioned to lead in this new era.

Advancements in Technology:

Technological advancements, such as artificial intelligence and machine learning, present new opportunities for empathy-driven innovation. These technologies can analyze large datasets to identify patient trends and preferences, personalize treatment plans, and predict patient outcomes. Integrating these tools with empathetic leadership can lead to more precise and effective healthcare solutions.

Global Health Challenges:

Addressing global health challenges, such as pandemics and chronic diseases, requires a collaborative and empathetic approach.

Indian pharmaceutical companies have the opportunity to leverage their expertise in generic medicines and biosimilars to provide affordable and accessible treatments worldwide. By focusing on empathy, companies can develop solutions that meet the diverse needs of global populations.

Policy and Advocacy:

Advocating for policies that support empathy-driven innovation will be essential for the future of Indian pharma. Pharmaceutical companies can work with regulators and policymakers to create an environment that incentivizes patient-centered research and development. This includes initiatives to streamline regulatory pathways for empathetic solutions and increase funding for patient engagement activities.

While implementing empathy-driven innovation in the pharmaceutical industry poses challenges, it is to be noted that the opportunities for growth and impact are substantial. Empathy will continue to play a pivotal role in shaping the future of Indian pharma innovation, ensuring a patient-centric approach that benefits all stakeholders.

Empathy-driven initiatives have the transformative potential to revolutionize the pharmaceutical industry by placing patients at the center of innovation. By understanding and addressing patient needs, pharmaceutical companies can develop more effective, safer, and accessible treatments.

This approach not only improves patient outcomes but also enhances customer loyalty, drives innovation, and strengthens employee engagement. The integration of empathy into organizational culture fosters collaboration, creativity, and a commitment to ethical practices. As a result, empathetic leadership becomes a catalyst for positive change across the healthcare ecosystem.

Empathy-driven innovation is not just about meeting regulatory requirements or achieving business objectives; it is about making a meaningful impact on people's lives. When patients feel understood, valued, and supported, they are more likely to adhere to treatment plans and experience better health outcomes. This, in turn, reduces the overall burden of disease and improves public health outcomes at a population level.

Together, we can create a future where patient needs are at the heart of every pharmaceutical decision, leading to better health outcomes and a more compassionate healthcare system.

Chapter 5
Integrity in Ethics: Guiding Principles in Indian Pharma

Integrity and ethics are foundational principles in the pharmaceutical industry, guiding the behavior and decisions of companies involved in developing, manufacturing, and distributing medications. In the Indian pharmaceutical landscape, these principles are particularly critical due to the unique challenges the industry faces, such as drug pricing, access to medications, and regulatory compliance.

Ethical practices ensure that companies prioritize patient safety and public trust, which are essential in an industry directly impacting human health. Maintaining high ethical standards is not only a moral obligation but also a strategic necessity for long-term success and reputation. In a market characterized by socio-economic disparities and varying access to healthcare, ethical decision-making can bridge gaps, foster innovation, and enhance patient outcomes.

This chapter delves into the importance of integrity and ethics in the Indian pharmaceutical industry. It explores the ethical challenges unique to this sector and underscores the need for a robust ethical framework. The chapter aims to provide a comprehensive understanding of how Indian pharma can navigate its complex landscape with integrity, ensuring that its operations contribute positively to society while achieving business objectives.

The purpose of this chapter is to delve into the critical role of integrity and ethics within the Indian pharmaceutical industry, highlighting the unique ethical challenges it faces. The chapter aims to underscore the importance of implementing a strong ethical framework to ensure that the industry operates in a way that prioritizes patient welfare, maintains public trust, and upholds social responsibility.

The chapter is organized into several main sections to provide a comprehensive analysis

Section I: The Ethical Landscape of the Indian Pharmaceutical Industry

Historical Context: Overview of the Development of the Pharmaceutical Industry in India

The pharmaceutical industry in India has undergone a remarkable transformation since its inception. In the early 20th century, the sector was dominated by multinational companies, with limited indigenous production capabilities. Post-independence, the Indian government took significant steps to develop a self-reliant pharmaceutical industry, emphasizing the need to produce essential drugs domestically. This legislative change spurred the growth of numerous domestic pharmaceutical companies, leading to a competitive market that prioritized affordability and accessibility. Companies such as Cipla, Zydus Cadila , Ranbaxy, and Dr. Reddy's Laboratories emerged as leaders in the industry, focusing on the production of generic drugs. The economic liberalization policies of the 1990s further accelerated growth, attracting foreign investment and fostering collaborations with global pharmaceutical giants.

Over the decades, the Indian pharmaceutical industry has evolved into a global powerhouse, renowned for its cost-effective generic drug production and significant contributions to global healthcare. India's role as the "pharmacy of the world" became evident during the early 2000s, when Indian companies supplied affordable antiretroviral drugs to developing countries, saving millions of lives.

Today, the industry is characterized by a robust research and development ecosystem, with increasing investments in innovation and biotechnology. However, the rapid growth and globalization of the industry have also brought forth numerous ethical challenges, necessitating a strong focus on integrity and ethical practices to navigate the complex landscape of pharmaceutical manufacturing, distribution, and regulation in India.

Key Milestones and Turning Points Shaping the Ethical Landscape of the Indian Pharmaceutical Industry

Several key milestones and turning points have profoundly influenced the ethical landscape of the Indian pharmaceutical industry, reflecting its dynamic evolution and the continuous need for integrity and ethical practices.

1. **Patents Act of 1970**:

   This act was a significant milestone, allowing the production of generic versions of patented drugs. While it democratized access to essential medications, it also posed ethical questions regarding intellectual property rights and the balance between innovation and accessibility.

2. **Economic Liberalization in the 1990s**:

   The liberalization policies opened the Indian market to global competition, increasing foreign investments and fostering collaborations with multinational companies. This period marked a shift towards higher standards in manufacturing practices but also raised concerns about maintaining ethical standards amidst rapid commercialization.

3. **HIV/AIDS Crisis and the Global Role of Indian Pharma**:

   During the early 2000s, Indian pharmaceutical companies played a crucial role in addressing the global HIV/AIDS crisis by providing affordable antiretroviral drugs. This era highlighted India's ethical responsibility to global health but also exposed the industry to scrutiny regarding the quality and efficacy of generic medications.

4. **Regulatory Reforms and Establishment of CDSCO**:

The establishment of the Central Drugs Standard Control Organization (CDSCO) aimed to enhance regulatory oversight and ensure compliance with international standards. However, challenges in regulatory enforcement and instances of non-compliance have raised ethical concerns about drug safety and efficacy.

5. **Emergence of Biopharmaceuticals and Biotechnology**:

   The shift towards biopharmaceuticals and biotechnology has brought about new ethical dilemmas, including issues related to clinical trials, patient consent, and the equitable distribution of advanced therapies.

These milestones have collectively shaped the ethical landscape of the Indian pharmaceutical industry, underscoring the need for a robust ethical framework to navigate the complex interplay between innovation, accessibility, and regulatory compliance.

Cultural and Social Influences on Business Ethics in the Indian Pharmaceutical Industry

Indian cultural and social values have a profound impact on business ethics within the pharmaceutical industry. These values, deeply rooted in India's diverse and complex societal fabric, influence how business is conducted and perceived at multiple levels.

1. **Respect for Authority and Hierarchy**: Indian culture traditionally places a high value on respect for authority and hierarchy, which can influence corporate structures and decision-making processes. This cultural aspect often translates into a top-down approach in business operations, where senior leaders play a pivotal role in setting ethical standards and practices. However, this respect for hierarchy can sometimes stifle dissent and inhibit open discussions

about ethical concerns, necessitating proactive efforts to encourage a culture of transparency and ethical dialogue.

2. Community Orientation and Social Responsibility: Indian society emphasizes collectivism and social responsibility. This cultural trait manifests in the pharmaceutical industry's focus on corporate social responsibility (CSR) initiatives aimed at improving community health and well-being. Companies often engage in activities such as setting up healthcare camps, supporting rural health programs, and providing affordable medications. The underlying principle is that businesses should contribute positively to society, reflecting the cultural ethos of 'seva' (service).

3. Ethical and Moral Values: Indian philosophy and religious teachings, which emphasize Dharma (duty) and Ahinsa (non-violence), significantly influence business ethics. These values encourage companies to act with integrity, avoid harm, and prioritize the well-being of all stakeholders, including patients, employees, and the broader community. Ethical business practices are not just seen as compliance with regulations but as a moral duty.

4. Familial Ties and Relationship Building: Strong familial ties and relationship-building are central to Indian culture. This translates into business practices where long-term relationships and trust are highly valued. Ethical behavior is crucial in maintaining these relationships, as unethical practices can lead to loss of trust and damage to reputations built over generations.

5. Ethical Dilemmas: While Indian culture promotes high ethical standards, the reality presents significant ethical challenges. Businesses often have to balance cultural expectations of integrity with the practicalities of operation.

Indian cultural and social values deeply influence business ethics in the pharmaceutical industry, promoting a blend of respect, social responsibility, moral integrity, and relationship-building.

Influence of Traditional Values on Ethical Decision-Making in the Pharmaceutical Sector

Traditional Indian values profoundly shape ethical decision-making in the pharmaceutical sector. One of the core values is **Dharma**, which signifies duty, righteousness, and moral responsibility. Pharmaceutical leaders who embrace this value prioritize ethical obligations over mere profit. This can be seen in their commitment to producing high-quality medications, even if it means incurring higher costs, and in their dedication to making essential drugs affordable for the masses.

The principle of **Ahinsa** (non-violence) also plays a crucial role. In the context of pharmaceuticals, ahinsa translates to ensuring that products are safe and that clinical trials are conducted ethically. Companies influenced by this value are likely to adopt rigorous safety standards, avoid harmful substances, and ensure that their practices do not exploit or harm vulnerable populations.

Seva (service) is another traditional value that drives ethical behavior. Pharmaceutical companies often engage in community service, such as organizing free health camps, supporting rural health initiatives, and donating medicines. These actions stem from a cultural emphasis on helping others and improving societal welfare.

The value of **Satyam** (truth) reinforces transparency and honesty in business practices. Ethical decision-making influenced by satyam involves maintaining transparency with stakeholders, including patients, healthcare providers, and regulators. This can manifest in clear labeling of products, honest reporting of clinical trial results, and straightforward communication regarding drug efficacy and safety.

Additionally, the collectivist nature of Indian society emphasizes **community well-being** over individual gain. This cultural aspect encourages pharmaceutical companies to consider the broader impact of their decisions on society. For instance, companies might prioritize the production of life-saving medications for widespread diseases, even if these are not the most profitable ventures.

Traditional Indian values like dharma, ahinsa, seva, satyam, and community well-being deeply influence ethical decision-making in the pharmaceutical sector, driving companies to operate with integrity, prioritize safety, and contribute positively to societal health.

Legal and Regulatory Framework:

The legal and regulatory framework governing ethics in the Indian pharmaceutical industry is crucial for ensuring the safety, efficacy, and ethical standards of drugs. It has evolved significantly over time to address emerging ethical concerns, improve transparency, and uphold public trust. Here's an overview of the laws and their evolution:

1. **Drugs and Cosmetics Act, 1940:** The Drugs and Cosmetics Act, 1940, and the rules made thereunder are the primary regulatory framework governing the manufacture, sale, and distribution of drugs in India. This Act provides provisions for the regulation of import, manufacture, distribution, and sale of drugs. It also mandates standards for the quality of drugs, medical devices, cosmetics, and diagnostics.
2. **Amendments and Additions:** Over the years, several amendments have been made to the Drugs and Cosmetics Act to strengthen its regulatory provisions:
   - **Drugs and Cosmetics (Amendment) Act, 1962:** This amendment introduced stricter provisions for drug licensing, import regulations, and quality standards.
   - **Drugs and Magic Remedies (Objectionable Advertisements) Act, 1954:** This Act prohibits

misleading advertisements related to drugs, claiming magical or miraculous cures.

- **Medical Devices Rules, 2017:** These rules were introduced to regulate medical devices separately from drugs, ensuring their safety and efficacy.
- **New Drugs and Clinical Trials Rules, 2019:** These rules replaced the earlier rules and aimed to streamline the approval process for new drugs and clinical trials, focusing on patient safety and ethical considerations.

3. **Central Drugs Standard Control Organization (CDSCO):** CDSCO, established under the Drugs and Cosmetics Act, is the national regulatory body for pharmaceuticals and medical devices. It is responsible for approving new drugs, regulating clinical trials, and ensuring compliance with quality standards. CDSCO plays a pivotal role in implementing the regulatory framework and monitoring the pharmaceutical industry.
4. **Evolution to Address Ethical Concerns:** The evolution of the regulatory framework in India has been driven by the need to address ethical concerns and improve patient safety:
   - **Stringent Clinical Trial Regulations:** The New Drugs and Clinical Trials Rules, 2019, introduced comprehensive guidelines for conducting clinical trials, emphasizing patient rights, informed consent, and monitoring of adverse events.
   - **Good Manufacturing Practices (GMP):** These practices ensure that pharmaceutical products are consistently produced and controlled according to quality standards. GMP guidelines have evolved to encompass international best practices, ensuring ethical manufacturing processes.
   - **Ethical Marketing Practices:** The regulations also cover ethical practices in the marketing and promotion of pharmaceutical products, prohibiting misleading claims and ensuring transparency.

- **Adoption of International Standards:** India has harmonized its regulatory standards with international guidelines, such as those issued by the International Council for Harmonisation (ICH), to align with global best practices in drug development and regulation.

5. **Challenges and Future Directions:** Despite the progress, challenges remain, including regulatory compliance issues, enforcement gaps, and the need for capacity building. Future directions include enhancing regulatory capacity, strengthening enforcement mechanisms, and promoting innovation while maintaining ethical standards.

The legal and regulatory framework governing ethics in the Indian pharmaceutical industry has evolved significantly to address ethical concerns, improve patient safety, and uphold public trust. The amendments and additions to the Drugs and Cosmetics Act, along with the establishment of CDSCO and stringent regulations for clinical trials and manufacturing practices, reflect India's commitment to maintaining high ethical standards in pharmaceuticals.

Public Perception and Trust:

Public perception of the pharmaceutical industry in India is influenced by a variety of factors, ranging from affordability and accessibility of medicines to concerns about ethics and transparency. Understanding how the public views the industry is crucial for maintaining trust and addressing ethical challenges effectively.

1. **Public Perception of the Pharmaceutical Industry:** The public perception of the pharmaceutical industry in India is mixed and influenced by several key factors:
    - **Affordability and Accessibility:** Many Indians rely on pharmaceutical products for their health needs, and affordability plays a critical role in their perception. The cost of medicines, especially essential drugs, often dictates public opinion. High prices can lead to

skepticism about the industry's intentions, while efforts to provide affordable medicines are viewed positively.

- **Quality and Safety:** There have been concerns about the quality and safety of pharmaceutical products in India, particularly in the context of counterfeit drugs and substandard medicines. Instances of quality issues can erode public trust and raise questions about regulatory oversight.
- **Ethical Practices:** Public perception also hinges on ethical practices within the industry, such as transparency in clinical trials, ethical marketing practices, and corporate social responsibility initiatives. Instances of unethical behavior, such as misleading advertising or inadequate safety disclosures, can damage the industry's reputation.
- **Innovation and R&D:** Positive perceptions are associated with pharmaceutical innovation, including the development of new drugs and medical technologies. Contributions to public health through research and development (R&D) are generally appreciated by the public.

2. **Role of Media and Public Opinion:** The media plays a significant role in shaping public perception and influencing ethical standards in the pharmaceutical industry:
    - **Reporting on Issues:** Media coverage often highlights issues such as drug pricing controversies, safety concerns, regulatory violations, and unethical practices. Negative reporting can contribute to public distrust and prompt regulatory actions.
    - **Public Discourse:** Media coverage fosters public discourse on healthcare issues, including drug access, patient rights, and industry practices. This discourse can influence policymakers and regulatory authorities to implement stricter ethical standards.

- **Advocacy and Awareness:** Media advocacy and investigative journalism raise awareness about ethical lapses and promote accountability within the industry. Public opinion, informed by media coverage, can pressure pharmaceutical companies to adopt more ethical practices.
- **Transparency and Accountability:** Increased media scrutiny encourages transparency and accountability in pharmaceutical operations. Companies that maintain open communication and engage with stakeholders proactively tend to enjoy more positive public perceptions.

Public perception of the pharmaceutical industry in India is shaped by affordability, quality, ethics, and innovation. The media plays a crucial role in influencing public opinion and advocating for ethical standards. For the industry to maintain public trust and credibility, it is essential to prioritize transparency, affordability, ethical practices, and patient safety in all operations. Collaboration between industry stakeholders, regulatory bodies, and the media can contribute to building a positive perception and ensuring ethical standards are upheld.

Comparative Analysis:

Comparative analysis of ethical practices in the Indian pharmaceutical industry with those in other countries reveals both similarities and differences, offering valuable lessons for improvement and adaptation.

1. **Lessons from Global Counterparts:**
    - **United States:** The U.S. pharmaceutical industry operates under stringent regulatory oversight, particularly in terms of drug approval and marketing. The Food and Drug Administration (FDA) plays a critical role in ensuring the safety and efficacy of drugs, although pricing remains a contentious issue.
    - **European Union:** The EU emphasizes transparency, patient safety, and ethical practices in pharmaceutical

operations. There is a strong focus on pharmacovigilance, ensuring that medicines marketed in the EU are continuously monitored for their safety profile.

   - **Japan:** Japan has a well-regulated pharmaceutical market with a strong emphasis on quality and patient safety. The Pharmaceuticals and Medical Devices Agency (PMDA) oversees drug approvals and ensures rigorous standards for clinical trials.
   - **Australia:** Australia has a comprehensive regulatory framework that emphasizes patient safety and efficacy. The Therapeutic Goods Administration (TGA) ensures that pharmaceutical products meet stringent quality standards and undergo thorough evaluation before market approval.

2. **Applicability in India:**
   - **Enhanced Regulatory Oversight:** India can benefit from strengthening regulatory oversight, improving enforcement mechanisms, and addressing regulatory gaps. Lessons from global counterparts, particularly in terms of transparency and pharmacovigilance, can inform regulatory reforms.
   - **Ethical Clinical Trials:** Improving ethical standards for clinical trials, including informed consent procedures, participant compensation, and transparency in reporting, is crucial. Adopting best practices from countries like the U.S. and EU can enhance India's clinical trial ecosystem.
   - **Marketing Guidelines:** Strengthening guidelines for pharmaceutical marketing practices.
   - **Access to Medicines:** India can continue to leverage its strengths in generic drug manufacturing to improve access to essential medicines. Balancing affordability with quality and safety standards is essential.

The Indian pharmaceutical industry can learn valuable lessons from global counterparts to enhance ethical practices. Strengthening regulatory oversight, improving clinical trial ethics, enhancing marketing guidelines, and ensuring access to medicines are key areas where India can benefit from global experiences. Collaborative efforts between industry stakeholders, regulatory authorities, and global counterparts can foster ethical standards that prioritize patient safety, transparency, and public trust.

Section II: Importance of an Ethical Framework in Indian Pharma

Defining an Ethical Framework:

An ethical framework in the pharmaceutical industry establishes the principles, values, and guidelines that guide the conduct of companies, healthcare professionals, and other stakeholders. It defines the standards for ethical behavior, ensuring that decisions and actions are aligned with moral principles and societal expectations. In India, where the pharmaceutical industry plays a critical role in public health, an ethical framework is essential to maintain trust, ensure patient safety, and uphold the integrity of the healthcare system.

Key Components of an Ethical Framework:

1. **Transparency:** Transparency is a fundamental aspect of an ethical framework. It involves openness in communication, decision-making processes, and interactions with stakeholders. In the pharmaceutical industry, transparency ensures that information about clinical trials, drug safety, pricing, and marketing practices is readily accessible to healthcare professionals, patients, and regulatory authorities. This transparency fosters trust and accountability, helping to mitigate conflicts of interest and unethical practices.
2. **Accountability:** Accountability holds individuals and organizations responsible for their actions and decisions. In the pharmaceutical context, accountability means taking ownership of outcomes, complying with regulations, and adhering to ethical standards. It involves identifying and rectifying mistakes, ensuring that processes are in place to prevent misconduct, and accepting consequences for unethical behavior. Accountability is crucial for maintaining public trust and ensuring that patient safety and well-being are prioritized.
3. **Fairness:** Fairness entails treating all stakeholders equitably and justly. In the pharmaceutical industry, fairness is demonstrated through fair pricing of medicines, equitable

access to healthcare, and unbiased treatment of patients and employees. Fairness also involves respecting the rights of patients in clinical trials, ensuring that vulnerable populations are protected, and promoting diversity and inclusion in the workforce. Fairness fosters a positive organizational culture and helps to build strong relationships with stakeholders.

4. **Integrity:** Integrity is the adherence to moral and ethical principles, even in the face of challenges or pressures. In the pharmaceutical industry, integrity means conducting business honestly, ethically, and with a commitment to high standards of professionalism. It involves avoiding conflicts of interest, maintaining confidentiality, and upholding the values of honesty and trustworthiness. Integrity is essential for building a reputable brand, attracting talent, and maintaining long-term relationships with stakeholders.
5. **Compliance with Laws and Regulations:** Adherence to laws and regulations is a cornerstone of an ethical framework. The pharmaceutical industry is heavily regulated to ensure patient safety, drug efficacy, and fair market practices. Compliance involves understanding and complying with laws related to drug development, manufacturing, distribution, marketing, and sales. It also includes maintaining accurate records, submitting required reports to regulatory agencies, and cooperating with inspections and audits. Compliance ensures that companies operate ethically within legal boundaries, protecting public health and safety.

An ethical framework in the Indian pharmaceutical industry is essential for promoting transparency, accountability, fairness, integrity, and compliance with laws and regulations. These components collectively ensure that the industry operates ethically, maintains public trust, and prioritizes patient welfare. Implementing and adhering to an ethical framework helps pharmaceutical companies navigate complex challenges, build strong relationships with stakeholders, and contribute positively to healthcare advancements.

The Role of Ethics in Building Trust

Ethical practices play a crucial role in building trust among stakeholders in the pharmaceutical industry, including patients, healthcare providers, and regulators. Here's how ethical standards contribute to trust and the long-term benefits of maintaining high ethical standards:

1. **Building Trust among Stakeholders:**

a. **Patients:** Ethical practices ensure that patient welfare is prioritized. This includes conducting clinical trials with integrity, providing accurate and transparent information about medications, and ensuring fair pricing and access to treatments. When patients perceive that their health and well-being are the primary concerns of pharmaceutical companies, trust is established. This trust encourages patient compliance with treatments, enhances patient satisfaction, and promotes loyalty to the brand.

b. **Healthcare Providers:** Ethical behavior in the pharmaceutical industry strengthens the relationship with healthcare providers. Providers rely on pharmaceutical companies for accurate information about drugs, their efficacy, and potential side effects. When companies uphold ethical standards, healthcare providers can confidently prescribe medications knowing they are safe and effective. This trust leads to better collaboration between pharmaceutical companies and healthcare professionals, improving patient care overall.

c. **Regulators:** Regulatory bodies play a critical role in ensuring the safety and efficacy of medications. Ethical practices, such as full compliance with regulations, accurate reporting of clinical trial data, and transparent communication, demonstrate a commitment to public health. When regulators trust that pharmaceutical companies are following ethical guidelines, they can focus on other areas of public health concern. This trust facilitates smoother regulatory processes, faster approvals for new drugs, and a more efficient healthcare system.

2. **Long-term Benefits of Maintaining High Ethical Standards:**

    a. **Reputation and Brand Loyalty:** Companies that prioritize ethics build a positive reputation and brand loyalty among patients, healthcare providers, and regulators. A strong reputation can differentiate a company from competitors and attract talented professionals and investors.

    b. **Sustainable Growth:** Ethical practices contribute to sustainable business growth by reducing legal and regulatory risks. Companies that comply with laws and regulations avoid costly fines and penalties, while maintaining ethical standards can lead to higher revenue and market share.

    c. **Employee Satisfaction and Retention:** Ethical companies foster a positive work environment that attracts and retains talented employees. Employees feel proud to work for a company that prioritizes patient welfare and ethical behavior, leading to higher job satisfaction and productivity.

    d. **Public Perception and Investor Confidence:** Ethical companies are viewed favorably by the public and investors. Investors are more likely to invest in companies with strong ethical principles, which can lead to increased funding for research and development and expansion opportunities.

Ethical practices in the pharmaceutical industry are essential for building trust among stakeholders, including patients, healthcare providers, and regulators. Maintaining high ethical standards leads to long-term benefits such as enhanced reputation, sustainable growth, employee satisfaction, and investor confidence. By prioritizing ethics, pharmaceutical companies contribute to a healthier society and improve overall patient outcomes.

Ethics and Corporate Social Responsibility (CSR) in the Pharmaceutical Industry

Ethics and Corporate Social Responsibility (CSR) are closely intertwined in the pharmaceutical industry, where companies are not only responsible for producing safe and effective medications but also for contributing positively to society. Here's how ethics and CSR are connected, along with examples of CSR initiatives by Indian pharmaceutical companies and their impact:

Relationship between Ethics and CSR:

Ethics in the pharmaceutical industry are the guiding principles that ensure companies operate with integrity, transparency, and respect for all stakeholders, including patients, healthcare providers, and the community at large. These ethical principles form the foundation on which CSR initiatives are built. CSR goes beyond legal obligations and compliance; it involves voluntary actions that benefit society and contribute to sustainable development.

In the pharmaceutical sector, CSR initiatives often focus on improving access to healthcare, supporting medical research and education, and promoting environmental sustainability. By engaging in CSR activities, companies demonstrate their commitment to ethical behavior and social responsibility, thereby enhancing their reputation and trustworthiness.

Impact of CSR on Company Reputation and Community Relations:

CSR initiatives have a significant impact on company reputation and community relations in the pharmaceutical industry:

1. **Enhanced Reputation:** Companies that engage in meaningful CSR initiatives build a positive reputation as responsible corporate citizens. This enhances their brand image and differentiates them from competitors.

2. **Improved Community Relations:** CSR activities contribute to stronger relationships with local communities by addressing their healthcare and educational needs. This fosters goodwill and trust among community members, which is crucial for long-term business success.

3. **Employee Engagement:** CSR initiatives also benefit employee morale and engagement. Employees feel proud to work for a company that contributes positively to society, which can lead to higher job satisfaction and productivity.

4. **Regulatory Compliance and Risk Management:** Engaging in CSR activities demonstrates a commitment to ethical behavior and social responsibility, which can help companies navigate regulatory challenges and mitigate risks.

Ethics and CSR are integral to the pharmaceutical industry, shaping companies' reputations and community relations. Indian pharmaceutical companies, such as Zydus Cadila , Dr. Reddy's Laboratories, Cipla, and Sun Pharmaceuticals, have demonstrated their commitment to CSR through initiatives that improve healthcare access, support education, and promote community welfare. These initiatives not only benefit society but also enhance company reputation, employee engagement, and long-term sustainability.

Section III: Strategies for Maintaining Integrity in Indian Pharma

Leadership and Ethical Culture in Indian Pharma

In the Indian pharmaceutical industry, leadership plays a crucial role in fostering an ethical culture within organizations. Ethical leadership is not only about compliance with laws and regulations but also about creating a culture where ethical behavior is ingrained in the company's values and practices. Here's how leadership contributes to ethical culture and examples of ethical leadership practices in Indian pharma companies:

Role of Leadership in Fostering Ethical Culture:

Leadership sets the tone for ethical behavior within an organization. Leaders who prioritize ethics demonstrate their commitment through actions and decisions, influencing employees to follow suit. They create an environment where ethical considerations are part of everyday decision-making processes. This includes promoting transparency, accountability, and fairness in all aspects of the business.

In the Indian pharmaceutical industry, ethical leadership is essential due to the sector's impact on public health and the high regulatory scrutiny it faces. Leaders must navigate complex ethical dilemmas related to drug pricing, access to medicines, clinical trials, and marketing practices. Ethical leaders ensure that these decisions are made with integrity, keeping the best interests of patients and stakeholders in mind.

Indian pharmaceutical companies often conduct regular ethics training sessions for employees at all levels. These sessions cover topics such as conflicts of interest, patient confidentiality, data integrity, and interactions with healthcare professionals. They also emphasize the company's commitment to ethical conduct and the consequences of unethical behavior.

Moreover, leadership development programs include modules on ethical leadership, where future leaders are trained to integrate ethics into their decision-making processes. This ensures that ethical culture is sustained and reinforced as new leaders take on roles of greater responsibility within the organization.

Leadership in Indian pharma plays a critical role in fostering an ethical culture. Through their actions and decisions, leaders set the tone for ethical behavior and create an environment where employees are empowered to act with integrity. Training and development programs further support this effort by educating employees on ethical standards and promoting a culture of compliance and responsibility.

Transparent Operations and Reporting in Indian Pharma

Importance of Transparency:

Transparency in operations and financial reporting is crucial in the pharmaceutical industry, particularly in India, due to its impact on public health and regulatory compliance. Here's why transparency is important and the mechanisms used to ensure it:

1. Importance of Transparency:

Transparency ensures that pharmaceutical companies operate with integrity and accountability. It involves openness in disclosing information related to their operations, financial performance, and decision-making processes. In the context of Indian pharma, transparency is essential for building trust among stakeholders, including patients, healthcare providers, regulators, and investors.

For patients and healthcare providers, transparent operations mean they can trust that the medications they receive are safe, effective, and produced under ethical conditions. It also ensures that they have access to accurate information about the drugs they are prescribed. For regulators, transparency helps in monitoring compliance with laws and regulations, ensuring that pharmaceutical companies adhere to quality standards and ethical practices.

2. Mechanisms for Ensuring Transparency:

Several mechanisms are used to ensure transparency in operations and financial reporting:

- **Audits:** Regular internal and external audits are conducted to verify the accuracy of financial statements and ensure compliance with accounting standards. Internal audits are conducted by the company's own audit team, while external audits are performed by independent auditors.
- **Third-Party Reviews:** Pharmaceutical companies often engage third-party organizations to review their operations, practices, and financial reporting. These reviews provide an unbiased assessment and validate the company's adherence to ethical and regulatory standards.
- **Disclosure Policies:** Companies establish policies for disclosing information to stakeholders, including financial reports, clinical trial results, and interactions with healthcare professionals. These policies ensure that information is shared openly and in a timely manner.

3. Benefits of Transparent Operations:

Transparent operations offer several benefits to stakeholders:

- **Enhanced Trust:** Stakeholders, including patients, healthcare providers, and investors, are more likely to trust companies that operate transparently. This trust leads to stronger relationships and improved reputation.
- **Compliance:** Transparent operations facilitate compliance with regulatory requirements. By openly disclosing information, companies demonstrate their commitment to following regulations and ethical standards.
- **Investor Confidence:** Transparent financial reporting attracts investors who are reassured by the company's commitment to accountability and governance. It reduces the risk of financial mismanagement or unethical practices that could harm shareholder value.

Transparency in operations and financial reporting is essential for maintaining trust, ensuring compliance, and fostering investor confidence in the Indian pharmaceutical industry. It supports ethical behavior and accountability, contributing to the industry's overall integrity and reputation.

Stakeholder Engagement in Indian Pharma: Addressing Ethical Concerns

In the Indian pharmaceutical industry, effective stakeholder engagement is critical for addressing ethical concerns and ensuring transparency and accountability. Here's an explanation of strategies for engaging with stakeholders and building partnerships to enhance ethical practices:

1. Strategies for Engaging with Stakeholders:

Patients and Healthcare Providers: Engaging with patients and healthcare providers involves creating channels for open communication and feedback. Pharmaceutical companies can implement the following strategies:

- **Patient Advisory Panels:** Establishing panels of patients and patient advocates to provide insights on ethical issues and the impact of pharmaceutical products.
- **Educational Initiatives:** Providing educational materials and resources to patients and healthcare providers about drug safety, proper use, and potential side effects.
- **Patient Support Programs:** Developing programs that provide support beyond medications, including counseling, adherence support, and disease management.

Regulators: Engaging with regulators is crucial to ensure compliance with ethical standards and regulations. Strategies include:

- **Regular Communication:** Maintaining open lines of communication to discuss regulatory changes, compliance issues, and best practices.

- **Collaborative Workshops:** Hosting workshops and seminars to educate regulators on new products, research findings, and patient outcomes.
- **Ethics Training:** Providing training to regulators on ethical considerations in drug development, clinical trials, and marketing practices.

2. Building Partnerships and Collaborations:

Academic and Research Institutions: Collaborating with academic and research institutions helps in advancing ethical practices and innovation. Strategies include:

- **Joint Research Projects:** Partnering on research initiatives that focus on ethical drug development, clinical trials, and patient outcomes.
- **Ethics Committees:** Establishing joint ethics committees to review research protocols and ensure ethical conduct.

Non-Governmental Organizations (NGOs): Working with NGOs can enhance corporate social responsibility (CSR) efforts and community engagement. Strategies include:

- **CSR Programs:** Collaborating on initiatives that improve healthcare access, patient education, and public health awareness.
- **Advocacy Campaigns:** Partnering on advocacy campaigns to promote ethical practices and transparency in the pharmaceutical industry.

Industry Associations: Joining industry associations allows companies to exchange best practices and develop industry-wide standards. Strategies include:

- **Code of Ethics:** Developing and adhering to a code of ethics that guides member companies on ethical conduct and compliance.

- **Ethics Forums:** Participating in forums that discuss emerging ethical issues, regulatory updates, and industry trends.

Effective stakeholder engagement and building partnerships are essential for addressing ethical concerns in the Indian pharmaceutical industry. By fostering collaboration and transparency, companies can enhance their ethical practices, improve patient outcomes, and build trust with stakeholders. These strategies contribute to the industry's overall integrity and reputation, ensuring sustainable growth and positive societal impact.

Regulatory and Compliance Programs in Indian Pharma

Overview of Regulatory and Compliance Programs:

In the Indian pharmaceutical industry, regulatory and compliance programs are essential for upholding ethical standards and ensuring adherence to legal requirements. These programs are designed to mitigate risks, ensure patient safety, and maintain the integrity of pharmaceutical products. Key regulatory bodies in India include the Central Drugs Standard Control Organization (CDSCO), which regulates the import, manufacture, distribution, and sale of drugs in the country, and the Drug Controller General of India (DCGI), responsible for approving licenses to manufacture drugs and ensuring compliance with drug regulations.

Best Practices for Maintaining Compliance:

1. **Comprehensive Regulatory Knowledge:** Pharmaceutical companies must stay updated with evolving regulatory requirements and guidelines. This includes understanding regulatory changes, updates in drug approval processes, and compliance with pharmacovigilance and clinical trial regulations.
2. **Internal Compliance Teams:** Companies should establish robust internal compliance teams comprising qualified professionals who oversee adherence to regulatory requirements. These teams are responsible for conducting

internal audits, monitoring operations, and ensuring that company practices align with ethical and legal standards.

3. **External Audits:** External audits by third-party firms or regulatory agencies play a crucial role in assessing compliance with ethical and regulatory standards. These audits help identify gaps, ensure transparency, and maintain accountability. They cover various aspects, including manufacturing practices, quality control, clinical trial protocols, and marketing practices.
4. **Ethics and Compliance Training:** Conducting regular ethics and compliance training programs for employees is essential. These programs educate staff about ethical considerations, regulatory requirements, and the importance of maintaining high standards of integrity in all operations.
5. **Documented Procedures and Policies:** Maintaining well-documented procedures and policies ensures clarity and consistency in compliance efforts. This includes documentation related to drug development, clinical trials, manufacturing processes, adverse event reporting, and marketing practices.

Role of Internal Compliance Teams and External Audits:

Internal compliance teams are responsible for:

- **Monitoring Operations:** Overseeing daily operations to ensure compliance with regulatory requirements and ethical standards.
- **Risk Assessment:** Identifying potential risks and implementing strategies to mitigate them.
- **Training and Education:** Providing ongoing training and education to employees on ethical conduct and regulatory compliance.
- **Reporting and Investigation:** Managing reporting mechanisms for potential violations and conducting investigations as needed.

External audits complement internal efforts by providing an independent assessment of compliance practices. These audits verify adherence to regulatory standards, assess risk management procedures, and ensure that ethical guidelines are followed throughout the organization. They play a crucial role in validating the effectiveness of internal compliance programs and enhancing transparency in pharmaceutical operations.

Regulatory and compliance programs are fundamental in maintaining ethical standards in the Indian pharmaceutical industry. By implementing best practices, leveraging internal compliance teams, conducting external audits, and providing ongoing training, companies can uphold integrity, ensure patient safety, and build trust with stakeholders. These efforts contribute to the industry's reputation and its ability to provide safe and effective healthcare solutions to the population.

Ethical Decision-Making Processes in Pharmaceutical Companies

Ethical decision-making in pharmaceutical companies involves navigating complex situations to ensure that actions are morally sound, comply with regulations, and prioritize patient well-being. Several frameworks and models exist to guide these processes, emphasizing transparency, accountability, and ethical behavior.

Frameworks and Models:

1. **Principles-Based Approach:** This approach relies on established ethical principles, such as beneficence (doing good), non-maleficence (doing no harm), justice, and autonomy. These principles help guide decisions related to patient care, drug development, and marketing practices.
2. **Ethical Decision-Making Models:**
    - **The Four-Component Model (Rest, 1986):** This model suggests that ethical decision-making involves four components: moral awareness, moral judgment, moral motivation, and moral action. It guides

individuals through a systematic process to evaluate ethical dilemmas.

    - **The Ethical Decision-Making Framework (Kidder, 1995):** This model offers a systematic approach with checkpoints to ensure ethical consistency in decision-making. It involves identifying the problem, gathering information, identifying ethical values, considering principles, and making a decision.

3. **Utilitarianism and Deontology:** These are philosophical approaches that assess the consequences of actions (utilitarianism) or adhere to rules and duties (deontology) to determine ethical outcomes.

Looking forward, ethics will play an increasingly pivotal role in shaping the future of the Indian pharmaceutical industry. As the industry continues to grow and evolve, maintaining high ethical standards will be crucial for sustaining trust among stakeholders, ensuring patient safety, and navigating regulatory complexities.

There will be an ongoing need for ethical innovation, where companies prioritize patient-centricity, transparency, and accountability in their practices. This includes ethical drug pricing, equitable access to medications, responsible marketing practices, and rigorous adherence to regulatory requirements.

Commitment to integrity will be a cornerstone of success, influencing decisions across all levels of the industry, from research and development to marketing and distribution. This dedication not only enhances corporate reputation but also fosters a culture of ethical leadership and responsibility.

In the future, ethical conduct will not only be a regulatory requirement but a strategic advantage, distinguishing companies that prioritize patient welfare and uphold ethical values from those that do not. As the Indian pharmaceutical industry continues to expand globally, maintaining ethical standards will be essential for long-term sustainability and growth.

Chapter 6
Building Trust through Community Engagement

Community engagement in the pharmaceutical industry involves actively collaborating with local populations to improve healthcare outcomes and address disparities. This chapter delves into the importance of such engagement, highlighting how pharmaceutical companies can play a pivotal role in enhancing public health by involving communities in their initiatives. By fostering strong relationships with the communities they serve, these companies can ensure that their efforts are more effective and aligned with the actual needs of the people.

Community involvement is crucial for addressing healthcare disparities, particularly in diverse and populous countries like India. Engaging with communities helps pharmaceutical companies understand the unique challenges and barriers faced by different groups, including access to medications, healthcare services, and health education. Through targeted initiatives such as health camps, mobile clinics, and public health education programs, pharmaceutical companies can directly address these issues, improving health outcomes and building trust with the community. Ultimately, a commitment to community engagement not only benefits public health but also enhances the reputation and sustainability of pharmaceutical companies, creating a positive impact that resonates beyond the corporate sphere. This chapter explores these themes, providing insights and examples of successful community-focused initiatives in the Indian pharmaceutical sector.

Section I: Understanding Community Engagement

Definition of Community Engagement in the Pharmaceutical Industry:

Community engagement in the pharmaceutical industry refers to the process by which pharmaceutical companies actively involve local communities in their initiatives aimed at improving public health. This involves a range of activities such as collaborating with local healthcare providers, conducting public health education campaigns, organizing health camps, and developing community-specific health programs. The goal is to build relationships with community members, understand their healthcare needs, and work together to create solutions that enhance health outcomes.

Importance of Community Engagement for Building Trust and Improving Public Health:

1. **Building Trust:**
   - **Transparency and Accountability:** By engaging with communities, pharmaceutical companies demonstrate transparency and accountability. This openness helps to build trust, as communities feel that their concerns and needs are being heard and addressed.
   - **Humanizing Corporate Entities:** Community engagement helps humanize pharmaceutical companies, transforming them from faceless entities into partners in health. This partnership fosters a sense of trust and mutual respect.
2. **Understanding Local Needs:**
   - **Tailored Solutions:** Engaging directly with communities allows pharmaceutical companies to gain a deeper understanding of the unique healthcare challenges faced by different populations. This knowledge enables the development of tailored solutions that are more effective and relevant.

- **Cultural Competence:** Community engagement promotes cultural competence within pharmaceutical companies. By interacting with diverse communities, companies can better appreciate and respect cultural differences, leading to more culturally sensitive healthcare initiatives.

3. **Improving Public Health:**
   - **Access to Healthcare:** Community engagement can help identify barriers to healthcare access and develop strategies to overcome them. For example, organizing mobile clinics in remote areas can provide much-needed medical services to underserved populations.
   - **Health Education:** Pharmaceutical companies can play a critical role in health education by conducting awareness campaigns and workshops. Educating communities about disease prevention, treatment options, and healthy lifestyle choices can lead to improved health outcomes.
   - **Partnerships with Local Providers:** By collaborating with local healthcare providers, pharmaceutical companies can enhance the delivery of healthcare services. These partnerships can lead to better coordination of care and more efficient use of resources.
4. **Corporate Social Responsibility (CSR):**
   - **Ethical Responsibility:** Community engagement aligns with the ethical responsibilities of pharmaceutical companies. It demonstrates a commitment to giving back to society and addressing social determinants of health.
   - **Reputation Management:** Companies that are actively involved in community engagement often enjoy a better reputation. Positive community relations can enhance the company's public image and foster goodwill.

Community engagement is a vital strategy for pharmaceutical companies aiming to build trust and improve public health. By actively involving communities in healthcare initiatives, companies can develop more effective, culturally sensitive solutions that address real needs, ultimately leading to better health outcomes and stronger community relationships.

Historical Context of Community Engagement in Indian Pharma

Overview of the Evolution of Community Engagement Practices in the Indian Pharmaceutical Sector:

Community engagement in the Indian pharmaceutical sector has evolved significantly over the decades, transitioning from basic charitable activities to comprehensive, strategic initiatives aimed at improving public health and fostering trust.

Early Years: Charitable Initiatives and Philanthropy

In the early years, community engagement by pharmaceutical companies in India was largely limited to philanthropic activities. Companies like GlaxoSmithKline (then Glaxo) and Alembic Pharmaceuticals focused on donations to hospitals, free medical camps, and sponsorships of health-related events. These initiatives were primarily aimed at addressing immediate healthcare needs and were more reactive than proactive.

1970s-1980s: Expansion of Healthcare Outreach

The 1970s and 1980s saw an expansion of healthcare outreach programs. The government's emphasis on primary healthcare and rural health led companies to align their initiatives with national health programs. For example, many pharmaceutical firms began supporting the government's efforts to eradicate diseases like smallpox and tuberculosis through the provision of vaccines and medicines at reduced costs or for free. This period marked the beginning of a more structured approach to community engagement, with companies recognizing the importance of being active participants in public health.

1990s: Formalization of Corporate Social Responsibility (CSR)

The 1990s were a turning point as corporate social responsibility (CSR) began to gain prominence. The liberalization of the Indian economy brought greater scrutiny on corporate practices, and there was a growing expectation for companies to contribute positively to society. This era saw pharmaceutical companies formalize their community engagement strategies, integrating them into broader CSR frameworks. Initiatives became more targeted and aligned with specific public health goals, such as maternal and child health, immunization drives, and health education.

2000s: Strategic and Sustainable Community Engagement

In the 2000s, the focus shifted towards strategic and sustainable community engagement. Companies like Dr. Reddy's Laboratories and Lupin Limited began implementing long-term projects aimed at addressing the root causes of health disparities. For instance, Lupin's Human Welfare & Research Foundation worked extensively on rural development programs, including healthcare, education, and livelihood projects, thereby addressing multiple determinants of health.

2010s-Present: Integrated Public Health Programs and Partnerships

The most recent phase, from the 2010s onwards, has seen the integration of community engagement into core business strategies. Companies are now partnering with non-governmental organizations (NGOs), government bodies, and international agencies to implement large-scale public health programs. Initiatives such as Sun Pharma's community health initiatives in tribal areas and Glenmark Pharmaceuticals' Project Kavach for maternal and child health are examples of how companies are using data-driven approaches to design and implement effective health interventions. These programs are often monitored and evaluated for impact, ensuring continuous improvement and sustainability.

Key Milestones and Turning Points:

- **1960s-1970s:** Early philanthropic efforts focusing on donations and medical camps.
- **1980s:** Alignment with national health programs, support for disease eradication efforts.
- **1990s:** Formalization of CSR, increased focus on structured and targeted health initiatives.
- **2000s:** Emphasis on strategic, long-term community engagement projects.
- **2010s-Present:** Integration of community engagement into core business strategies, focus on partnerships and sustainable impact.

This evolution reflects a growing understanding within the Indian pharmaceutical industry of the importance of community engagement not just as a corporate responsibility but as a strategic imperative that contributes to both public health and business success.

Section II: Community-Focused Initiatives in Indian Pharma

Health Camps and Mobile Clinics

Description of Initiatives

Health camps and mobile clinics are vital community-focused initiatives undertaken by Indian pharmaceutical companies to provide essential healthcare services to underserved areas. These initiatives are particularly significant in rural and remote regions where access to medical facilities is limited. Health camps typically involve temporary setups where healthcare professionals offer free medical check-ups, diagnostic services, and treatments for common ailments. Mobile clinics, on the other hand, are fully equipped medical vehicles that travel to remote locations, offering a range of healthcare services, including vaccinations, maternal and child health services, and chronic disease management.

Pharmaceutical companies collaborate with local health authorities, non-governmental organizations (NGOs), and community leaders to organize these camps and clinics. They deploy doctors, nurses, and healthcare workers who not only provide medical care but also educate community members on preventive healthcare practices, hygiene, and nutrition.

Impact on Community Health and Trust-Building

Health camps and mobile clinics have a profound impact on community health and trust-building. Firstly, they address the immediate healthcare needs of underserved populations by providing timely and accessible medical services. This intervention can lead to early diagnosis and treatment of diseases, reducing morbidity and mortality rates in these areas.

Secondly, these initiatives enhance community trust in pharmaceutical companies. By showing a commitment to improving local health outcomes, companies build a positive relationship with community members. This trust is crucial, as it can lead to increased acceptance of pharmaceutical products and health interventions promoted by the companies.

Furthermore, health camps and mobile clinics contribute to long-term public health by promoting health education and preventive care. Educated communities are more likely to adopt healthier lifestyles and seek timely medical attention, which can reduce the overall disease burden.

Health camps and mobile clinics are effective community-focused initiatives that improve health outcomes in underserved areas while fostering trust and goodwill between pharmaceutical companies and local communities.

Public Health Education Programs

Overview of Educational Programs

Public health education programs play a critical role in improving health literacy among communities, particularly in underserved areas. These programs are designed to raise awareness about various health issues, promote healthy behaviors, and empower individuals with the knowledge necessary to make informed health decisions. Pharmaceutical companies, in partnership with healthcare professionals, NGOs, and government agencies, implement these educational initiatives to address pressing public health concerns.

Examples of Initiatives

1. **Disease Prevention Campaigns**: Programs focused on educating the public about the prevention and management of communicable and non-communicable diseases, such as tuberculosis, diabetes, and hypertension. These campaigns often include workshops, informational pamphlets, and community meetings.

2. **Hygiene and Sanitation Programs**: Initiatives aimed at improving hygiene practices to prevent infectious diseases. These programs might involve training sessions on handwashing, safe drinking water practices, and proper waste disposal.
3. **Nutrition Education**: Programs that teach communities about balanced diets, the importance of vitamins and minerals, and healthy eating habits to combat malnutrition and lifestyle-related diseases.

Analysis of Outcomes and Effectiveness

Public health education programs have shown significant positive outcomes. They enhance community health literacy, leading to better health-seeking behaviors and adherence to medical advice. For example, disease prevention campaigns have led to increased rates of vaccination and early detection of chronic illnesses, thereby reducing the overall disease burden.

Hygiene and sanitation programs have resulted in noticeable improvements in public health, evidenced by lower incidences of waterborne and communicable diseases. Nutrition education initiatives have contributed to better dietary habits, reducing rates of malnutrition and obesity.

Effectiveness is often measured through pre- and post-program surveys, health indicators like disease incidence rates, and community feedback. Continuous monitoring and evaluation help in refining these programs to better meet the needs of the target populations.

Public health education programs by pharmaceutical companies significantly improve health literacy and community health outcomes, thereby fostering trust and collaboration between the industry and the communities they serve.

Collaborations with Non-Governmental Organizations (NGOs)

Discussion on Partnerships

Pharmaceutical companies often collaborate with non-governmental organizations (NGOs) to extend their reach and impact in underserved communities. These partnerships leverage the strengths and resources of both parties: pharmaceutical companies provide medical expertise, medications, and funding, while NGOs offer grassroots connections, local knowledge, and implementation capabilities. This synergy enhances the effectiveness of community health initiatives, ensuring that interventions are culturally appropriate and accessible.

Examples of Successful Collaborations

1. **The Partnership for Quality Medical Supplies**: A collaboration between a leading pharmaceutical company and a health-focused NGO that aims to provide high-quality medications and medical supplies to rural health centers. This partnership has significantly improved the availability of essential medicines in remote areas, thereby reducing mortality and morbidity from treatable conditions.
2. **Community Health Workers Program**: In this initiative, a pharmaceutical company collaborates with an NGO to train community health workers (CHWs) on disease prevention, maternal and child health, and chronic disease management. CHWs act as liaisons between the healthcare system and the community, facilitating better health outcomes through education and direct care.
3. **Disease Eradication Campaigns**: Collaborations targeting the eradication of specific diseases, such as tuberculosis or malaria, have been highly successful. Pharmaceutical companies provide the necessary medications and vaccines, while NGOs mobilize community members, conduct awareness campaigns, and ensure compliance with treatment protocols.

Impact on Community Health

These collaborations have led to significant improvements in community health metrics, such as increased immunization rates, better management of chronic diseases, and reduced incidence of infectious diseases. They also enhance community trust in pharmaceutical companies, as these partnerships demonstrate a commitment to social responsibility and public health beyond commercial interests. By working together, pharmaceutical companies and NGOs can create sustainable health solutions that are both impactful and scalable.

Local Employment and Economic Development Initiatives

Pharmaceutical companies in India have increasingly recognized the importance of contributing to local economies by providing employment opportunities and supporting economic development initiatives. These efforts not only enhance community well-being but also strengthen the company's social license to operate.

Initiatives Providing Employment Opportunities

1. **Local Hiring Practices**: Pharmaceutical companies prioritize hiring from local communities to ensure that economic benefits from their operations remain within the region. This approach not only creates job opportunities but also helps in reducing unemployment and poverty levels in the area.
2. **Skill Development Programs**: Companies often collaborate with local vocational training institutes or NGOs to provide training programs aimed at developing skills relevant to the pharmaceutical industry. These programs empower local residents with the skills needed to secure jobs within the company or in related sectors.
3. **Promotion of Small and Medium Enterprises (SMEs)**: Pharmaceutical companies support local SMEs by sourcing goods and services locally whenever possible. This practice boosts the local economy and encourages the growth of small businesses, which in turn creates more employment opportunities.

Economic Development Initiatives

1. **Infrastructure Development**: Some pharmaceutical companies invest in local infrastructure projects, such as building roads, schools, or health centers, which benefit the community and support economic growth.
2. **Entrepreneurship Support**: Companies may offer support to local entrepreneurs by providing access to business training, mentoring, and financial assistance to start or expand businesses.

Impact on Local Communities

These initiatives have a profound impact on local communities. They stimulate economic growth, improve living standards, and contribute to the overall socio-economic development of the region. By engaging with the local community in this way, pharmaceutical companies also foster goodwill and strengthen relationships, which is crucial for maintaining a positive corporate image and reputation.

Pharmaceutical companies that invest in local employment and economic development initiatives not only fulfill their corporate social responsibility but also create sustainable benefits for the communities in which they operate. These efforts contribute to inclusive growth and help build resilient and thriving communities.

Section III: The Impact of Community Engagement on Public Health

Improving Access to Healthcare

Community engagement initiatives by pharmaceutical companies in India play a crucial role in improving access to healthcare, particularly in remote and underserved areas. These initiatives are designed to address the barriers that prevent individuals from accessing necessary healthcare services, such as geographic isolation, economic constraints, and lack of awareness. By focusing on these communities, pharmaceutical companies can make a significant impact on public health outcomes.

Community Health Camps and Mobile Clinics

One of the primary methods used by pharmaceutical companies to improve healthcare access in remote areas is through health camps and mobile clinics. These initiatives involve setting up temporary healthcare facilities in underserved communities where residents can receive free or subsidized medical consultations, screenings, and medications. Health camps are often organized in collaboration with local healthcare providers or non-governmental organizations (NGOs) to ensure comprehensive care delivery.

Impact on Healthcare Access

These initiatives have shown tangible improvements in healthcare access in several ways:

1. **Increased Outreach**: Health camps and mobile clinics reach populations that are typically excluded from regular healthcare services due to geographical barriers. By bringing healthcare directly to these communities, pharmaceutical

companies ensure that individuals who would otherwise have limited or no access to medical care receive timely treatment.

2. **Early Detection and Treatment**: Through screenings and medical consultations, health camps enable early detection of health conditions such as diabetes, hypertension, and infectious diseases. Early detection allows for prompt treatment, which can prevent the progression of diseases and improve health outcomes.
3. **Medication Access**: Many health camps also provide free or subsidized medications to patients, addressing the issue of affordability. This is particularly beneficial in rural areas where purchasing medications can be a financial burden for low-income families.
4. **Health Education**: Alongside medical consultations, health camps often include health education sessions aimed at raising awareness about preventive measures, nutrition, hygiene practices, and disease management. This empowers communities to take control of their health and adopt healthier lifestyles.

Data Showing Improvements in Health Outcomes

Data collected from these initiatives consistently demonstrate positive health outcomes:

- **Reduction in Disease Burden**: Health camps and mobile clinics contribute to a reduction in the prevalence and severity of communicable and non-communicable diseases in the targeted communities.
- **Improved Maternal and Child Health**: Initiatives focused on maternal and child health improve prenatal care, childbirth practices, and childhood immunizations, leading to lower maternal and infant mortality rates.
- **Health Screenings**: Regular health screenings conducted during these camps help in the early detection of diseases, thereby reducing complications and improving treatment outcomes.

Community engagement initiatives such as health camps and mobile clinics are essential for bridging the gap in healthcare access in remote and underserved areas of India. They not only provide essential medical services but also contribute to improving health outcomes and enhancing the overall well-being of the population. By focusing on these initiatives, pharmaceutical companies demonstrate their commitment to corporate social responsibility and contribute significantly to public health improvement efforts.

Building Trust and Relationships with Communities

Building trust between pharmaceutical companies and communities is crucial for the success and sustainability of community engagement initiatives. Consistent and meaningful engagement plays a pivotal role in fostering trust, which is built over time through transparency, empathy, and delivering on promises. Here, we explore how pharmaceutical companies can effectively build trust and share stories and testimonials that highlight the impact of these efforts on community members.

Role of Consistent Engagement

Consistent engagement involves ongoing interactions and collaborations between pharmaceutical companies and communities. This engagement is not just about providing one-off services but about developing long-term relationships that are built on mutual respect and understanding. When pharmaceutical companies consistently engage with communities, it demonstrates a commitment to their well-being beyond mere business interests.

Transparency and Communication

Transparency is key to building trust. Pharmaceutical companies should communicate openly about their goals, actions, and outcomes of community engagement initiatives. This transparency helps to manage expectations and ensures that community members understand the company's motivations and the benefits they can expect. Clear and honest communication about challenges, setbacks, and successes also builds credibility and trust.

Empathy and Understanding

Empathy is another essential aspect of building trust. Pharmaceutical companies must demonstrate empathy by understanding the unique needs, challenges, and aspirations of the communities they serve. This understanding should inform the design and implementation of community engagement programs to ensure they are relevant and impactful.

Impact Stories and Testimonials

Stories and testimonials from community members are powerful tools to illustrate the impact of community engagement initiatives and to build trust. These narratives highlight real-life experiences, demonstrating how pharmaceutical companies have positively affected individuals and communities.

Examples and Testimonials:

- **Improved Healthcare Access:** Community members may share stories of how health camps or mobile clinics provided them with access to medical care they would otherwise not have received due to distance or financial constraints. Testimonials might include how early detection and treatment through these initiatives saved lives or improved health outcomes.
- **Health Education:** Individuals can recount how health education sessions helped them understand preventive healthcare measures, leading to healthier lifestyles and reduced incidence of disease in their families.
- **Economic Empowerment:** Testimonials might highlight how employment opportunities provided by pharmaceutical companies improved household incomes and quality of life in the community.

- **Environmental Impact:** Communities might share stories of how sustainability initiatives by pharmaceutical companies improved local environmental conditions, such as water purification projects or waste management programs.

These stories and testimonials serve as powerful evidence of the positive impact of pharmaceutical companies' community engagement efforts. They provide authentic, relatable accounts of how these initiatives have made a difference in the lives of community members, thus building trust and reinforcing the company's commitment to social responsibility.

Building trust and relationships with communities requires consistent, transparent, and empathetic engagement. By listening to community needs, communicating openly, and sharing impactful stories and testimonials, pharmaceutical companies can build trust, strengthen relationships, and ensure the long-term success of their community engagement initiatives. This trust is essential for creating sustainable positive impacts on public health and well-being.

Section IV: Strategies for Effective Community Engagement

Developing a Community Engagement Plan

Developing and implementing an effective community engagement plan is essential for pharmaceutical companies to establish meaningful relationships and foster trust with the communities they serve. Here are steps for creating and executing a successful community engagement plan:

1. **Assess Community Needs and Priorities:** Begin by conducting a thorough assessment of the community's needs, priorities, and challenges. This can involve community consultations, surveys, and interviews with key stakeholders such as community leaders, healthcare providers, and local authorities. Understanding these factors helps in tailoring engagement initiatives to address specific needs.
2. **Set Clear Objectives and Goals:** Define clear objectives and goals for the community engagement plan. These should align with the company's corporate social responsibility (CSR) strategy and the identified needs of the community. Goals could include improving healthcare access, enhancing health education, or supporting economic development.
3. **Develop Engagement Strategies:** Based on the identified needs and goals, develop strategies for engagement. This may include initiatives such as health camps, mobile clinics, educational workshops, or employment programs. Consideration should be given to cultural sensitivity and the unique characteristics of the community.
4. **Establish Communication Channels:** Create effective communication channels to engage with the community. This can include town hall meetings, focus group discussions, community forums, and digital platforms. Communication should be clear, transparent, and easily accessible to community members.

5. **Implement the Plan:** Execute the engagement plan in collaboration with community stakeholders and partners. Ensure that activities are well-organized, resources are allocated appropriately, and timelines are adhered to.
6. **Monitor and Evaluate:** Continuously monitor the progress and impact of community engagement initiatives. Collect feedback from community members, stakeholders, and participants to assess effectiveness and identify areas for improvement.
7. **Adapt and Improve:** Based on the evaluation findings, adapt the engagement strategies as needed to better meet community needs and achieve desired outcomes. Continuous improvement ensures that engagement efforts remain relevant and impactful.

Importance of Stakeholder Involvement and Feedback

Stakeholder involvement and feedback are critical components of effective community engagement. Involving stakeholders—such as community leaders, healthcare providers, NGOs, and local authorities—from the outset ensures that engagement efforts are well-informed and supported. Their involvement helps in understanding community dynamics, gaining local insights, and building trust.

Feedback from stakeholders and community members provides valuable insights into the effectiveness and impact of engagement initiatives. It allows for adjustments to be made in real-time, based on the needs and preferences of the community. Regular feedback mechanisms, such as surveys, focus groups, and community meetings, help in maintaining open lines of communication and fostering a sense of ownership among community members.

Developing a community engagement plan involves assessing community needs, setting clear objectives, developing strategies, establishing communication channels, implementing the plan, monitoring progress, and adapting based on feedback. Stakeholder involvement and feedback are integral to the success of these efforts, ensuring that engagement initiatives are relevant, effective, and sustainable. By following these steps and emphasizing stakeholder engagement, pharmaceutical companies can build meaningful relationships with communities and contribute to improving public health and well-being.

Building Partnerships and Collaborations

Building strong partnerships with community organizations, NGOs, and government bodies is crucial for pharmaceutical companies to effectively engage with communities and address healthcare challenges. Here are strategies for establishing and maintaining successful collaborations:

1. **Identify Common Goals and Objectives:** The first step in building partnerships is to identify common goals and objectives between the pharmaceutical company and the community organizations, NGOs, or government bodies. This involves understanding the needs and priorities of the community and aligning them with the company's CSR objectives. For example, both parties may share an interest in improving access to healthcare services in underserved areas.
2. **Develop Mutually Beneficial Relationships:** Successful partnerships are built on mutual benefit and reciprocity. Pharmaceutical companies can offer resources, expertise, and funding, while community organizations and NGOs provide local knowledge, trust, and access to communities. For instance, a company might collaborate with an NGO to implement health education programs or provide medical supplies to remote villages.
3. **Establish Clear Communication Channels:** Effective communication is essential for building and maintaining partnerships. Establish clear communication channels and maintain regular contact to ensure transparency and alignment of activities. This includes regular meetings, progress updates, and feedback sessions.

4. **Ensure Accountability and Commitment:** Both parties should commit to the partnership and hold each other accountable for agreed-upon activities and outcomes. This can be formalized through partnership agreements or memoranda of understanding (MOUs) that outline roles, responsibilities, and expectations.
5. **Cultural Sensitivity and Respect:** Respect for local culture, values, and customs is critical in building trust and maintaining successful partnerships. Pharmaceutical companies should demonstrate cultural sensitivity and adaptability in their engagement efforts.

Examples of Successful Collaborations:

1. **Novartis India and SNEHA (Society for Nutrition, Education and Health Action):** Novartis India collaborated with SNEHA to implement a maternal and child health program in urban slums of Mumbai. The program focused on improving maternal health outcomes through health education, antenatal care, and nutrition support.
2. **Pfizer and Operation Smile India:** Pfizer partnered with Operation Smile India to provide free cleft lip and palate surgeries to children from underserved communities across India. The partnership involved Pfizer providing financial support and medical volunteers, while Operation Smile India coordinated the surgeries and post-operative care.
3. **GSK and Save the Children India:** GSK collaborated with Save the Children India to address child malnutrition in the state of Uttar Pradesh. The partnership included community-based interventions, nutrition education, and training of healthcare workers to improve child health outcomes.

These collaborations demonstrate how pharmaceutical companies can leverage partnerships with community organizations, NGOs, and government bodies to address healthcare disparities, improve access to healthcare services, and build trust within communities. By working together towards shared goals, these partnerships contribute to sustainable social impact and positive health outcomes.

Sustaining Long-Term Engagement

Consistency and sustainability are key elements in maintaining effective community engagement efforts for pharmaceutical companies. Here's why they are important and tips for sustaining long-term relationships with communities:

Importance of Consistency and Sustainability:

Consistency in community engagement efforts ensures that pharmaceutical companies build trust and credibility within communities over time. It demonstrates a commitment to the community's well-being beyond short-term projects or initiatives. Sustainability, on the other hand, ensures that positive impacts continue to benefit communities over the long term. It involves implementing programs and initiatives that can be maintained and scaled up over time, contributing to lasting improvements in community health and well-being.

Tips for Maintaining Long-Term Relationships:

1. **Transparent Communication:** Open and transparent communication is essential for building and maintaining trust with communities. Keep community members informed about ongoing and future initiatives, progress, and outcomes. Solicit feedback and adapt strategies based on community needs and preferences.
2. **Cultural Sensitivity:** Respect and understanding of local culture, customs, and traditions are critical. Engage with community leaders and stakeholders to ensure that initiatives are culturally appropriate and respectful.
3. **Adaptability and Flexibility:** Communities evolve, and their needs may change over time. Stay adaptable and flexible in response to changing circumstances. Regularly reassess community needs and adjust engagement strategies as necessary.
4. **Collaboration and Partnership:** Build strong partnerships with local organizations, NGOs, and community leaders.

Collaborate on initiatives that are mutually beneficial and aligned with community priorities. Engaging local partners ensures that initiatives are sustainable and rooted in the community.

5. **Capacity Building:** Invest in building the capacity of local communities to participate in and lead health initiatives. Provide training, resources, and support to empower community members to take ownership of their health and well-being.
6. **Long-Term Commitment:** Community engagement should not be seen as a one-time effort but as a long-term commitment. Allocate resources and dedicate personnel to sustain engagement efforts over time.
7. **Measure and Communicate Impact:** Regularly assess the impact of community engagement efforts. Collect data on health outcomes, community satisfaction, and behavioral changes. Share successes and challenges with stakeholders to demonstrate the value of engagement efforts.

By prioritizing consistency, sustainability, and community involvement, pharmaceutical companies can build enduring relationships that contribute to improved health outcomes and strengthened community resilience. These efforts not only enhance corporate social responsibility but also foster a positive reputation and long-term success in the pharmaceutical industry.

Section V: Challenges and Opportunities in Community Engagement

Community engagement initiatives in the pharmaceutical industry can be transformative, but they also present several challenges. Overcoming these challenges and leveraging opportunities can lead to significant growth and innovation.

Common Challenges

1. **Resource Constraints:** Community engagement initiatives require substantial resources, including financial investments, human resources, and time. Many pharmaceutical companies face challenges in allocating sufficient resources to sustain long-term engagement efforts. Moreover, the COVID-19 pandemic has exacerbated these challenges, with limited budgets impacting the scope and scale of community programs.
   Strategies for Overcoming Resource Constraints:
   - **Partnerships and Collaboration:** Collaborate with NGOs, local healthcare providers, and government agencies to share resources and expertise.
   - **Leverage Technology:** Use digital tools for remote engagement and virtual healthcare services to reduce costs.
   - **Prioritize Impact:** Focus resources on initiatives with the highest potential for improving health outcomes and building community trust.
2. **Resistance from Communities:** Communities may exhibit resistance due to mistrust, cultural barriers, or misunderstanding of intentions. Pharmaceutical companies often face challenges in gaining acceptance and participation from community members.
   Strategies for Overcoming Community Resistance:
   - **Transparency and Communication:** Foster open dialogue and transparent communication about the

purpose, goals, and expected outcomes of engagement initiatives.
    - **Cultural Sensitivity:** Adapt initiatives to align with cultural values and practices of the community. Involve community leaders and stakeholders in decision-making processes.
    - **Long-Term Commitment:** Build trust through sustained engagement efforts that demonstrate a genuine commitment to community well-being.
3. **Regulatory and Compliance Issues:** Compliance with local regulations and ethical standards is crucial in community engagement efforts. Pharmaceutical companies must navigate complex regulatory landscapes, ensuring that initiatives adhere to legal requirements and ethical guidelines. **Strategies for Ensuring Compliance:**
    - **Legal Expertise:** Employ legal experts to navigate regulatory frameworks and ensure compliance with local laws.
    - **Ethical Guidelines:** Adhere to ethical guidelines and principles in all engagement activities, including data privacy, informed consent, and confidentiality.
    - **Regular Audits:** Conduct regular audits and reviews to monitor compliance and mitigate risks.

Opportunities for Growth and Innovation

1. **Innovative Healthcare Delivery Models:** Community engagement presents opportunities to innovate in healthcare delivery, particularly in remote and underserved areas. Initiatives such as mobile clinics, telemedicine, and health camps can improve access to healthcare services.
    - **Example:** Introducing mobile clinics equipped with diagnostic tools and staffed by healthcare professionals to provide essential healthcare services to remote communities.
2. **Building Brand Reputation:** Effective community engagement can enhance a pharmaceutical company's

reputation and brand image. By demonstrating commitment to community health and well-being, companies can build trust and credibility among stakeholders.

- **Example:** Implementing sustainable healthcare initiatives and educational programs that empower communities and improve health literacy.

3. **Driving Business Growth:** Community engagement initiatives have the potential to drive business growth by expanding market reach and enhancing market penetration. Companies that invest in community health and well-being may see increased demand for their products and services.
    - **Example:** Collaborating with local healthcare providers and NGOs to distribute medicines and promote disease awareness campaigns, thereby increasing market access.
4. **Enhancing Employee Engagement:** Engaging employees in community initiatives can boost morale, improve job satisfaction, and foster a sense of pride in the company's mission and values.
    - **Example:** Encouraging employees to volunteer in community health programs or participate in corporate social responsibility activities.
5. **Strategic Partnerships and Collaborations:** Forming partnerships with NGOs, government agencies, and community organizations can create synergies and amplify the impact of community engagement initiatives.
    - **Example:** Collaborating with a local NGO to launch a health education program aimed at preventing chronic diseases in urban slums.

While community engagement in the pharmaceutical industry poses challenges, it also presents significant opportunities for growth and innovation. By addressing resource constraints, overcoming community resistance, and ensuring regulatory compliance, pharmaceutical companies can harness the potential of community engagement to drive business growth, enhance reputation, and improve public health outcomes. Emphasizing long-term commitment, cultural sensitivity, and ethical conduct will be crucial in realizing these opportunities and building sustainable partnerships with communities.

Looking ahead, community engagement in the Indian pharmaceutical industry is poised to play an increasingly pivotal role. As healthcare systems continue to evolve and face new challenges, the importance of community involvement and support will only grow. Pharmaceutical companies have a unique opportunity to enhance their role as stakeholders in public health by investing in sustainable community engagement initiatives.

The future of community engagement in Indian pharma will likely see advancements in technology-driven healthcare delivery, such as telemedicine and digital health solutions. These innovations will help bridge gaps in healthcare access and empower communities with knowledge and resources. Moreover, there will be a greater emphasis on culturally sensitive and locally tailored programs that address the specific health needs and challenges of diverse populations across India.

It is essential for pharmaceutical companies to prioritize community engagement not only as a corporate social responsibility but also as a strategic imperative for business growth and reputation enhancement. By building trust, fostering partnerships, and contributing to community well-being, companies can create lasting impacts on public health while securing a sustainable future for themselves in the dynamic landscape of Indian pharma.

Chapter 7
Navigating Challenges with Resilience

The Indian pharmaceutical sector faces a myriad of challenges that threaten its growth and effectiveness. These challenges include regulatory complexities, intense market competition, and issues related to public perception and trust. Regulatory hurdles often complicate the process of bringing new drugs to market, while stringent international standards add another layer of difficulty. Market competition, both from domestic companies and international giants, demands continuous innovation and efficiency. Additionally, maintaining a positive public perception is crucial, as negative publicity can significantly impact a company's reputation and consumer trust.

Resilience and innovation are essential for navigating these challenges. Resilience enables companies to adapt to regulatory changes, market dynamics, and public scrutiny, ensuring their continued operation and success. Innovation drives the development of new products, processes, and strategies, allowing companies to stay competitive and meet the evolving needs of patients and healthcare providers. By fostering a culture of resilience and innovation, pharmaceutical companies can not only overcome current challenges but also position themselves for future success.

The purpose of this chapter is to analyze the major challenges faced by leaders in the Indian pharmaceutical sector and to explore how resilience and innovation can be leveraged to address these issues.

Major Challenges in the Indian Pharmaceutical Sector

Regulatory Complexities

The regulatory environment in India involves multiple agencies and stringent compliance requirements. The Central Drugs Standard Control Organization (CDSCO) is the primary regulatory body responsible for drug approval, regulation, and oversight. Additionally, the Drug Controller General of India (DCGI) plays role in ensuring that pharmaceutical products meet safety, efficacy, and quality standards. Regulations cover a broad spectrum, from clinical trials and manufacturing practices to marketing and distribution.

Challenges Related to Compliance with National and International Regulations

Compliance with both national and international regulations presents a significant challenge for Indian pharmaceutical companies. Nationally, companies must navigate an evolving regulatory landscape with frequent updates and amendments to laws and guidelines.

Internationally, Indian pharmaceutical companies aiming to export their products face additional layers of complexity.

Regulatory requirements differ across countries, and meeting the stringent standards of agencies like the U.S. Food and Drug Administration (FDA) and the European Medicines Agency (EMA) can be daunting. These regulations often demand extensive documentation, rigorous testing, and regular audits, which can strain resources and delay product launches.

Market Competition

Description of the Competitive Landscape in the Indian Pharmaceutical Market

The Indian pharmaceutical market is one of the most competitive globally. It is characterized by a large number of players ranging from multinational corporations to small and medium-sized enterprises. This intense competition is driven by several factors including- the country's role as a major generic drug manufacturer, the high demand for affordable medications, and the presence of a skilled workforce.

Challenges Posed by Both Domestic and International Competitors

1. **Domestic Competition:**
    - **Price Wars:** Indian pharmaceutical companies often engage in aggressive pricing strategies to capture market share. This leads to thin profit margins and intense competition.
    - **Quality and Innovation:** Domestic companies are continuously innovating to improve drug formulations and delivery mechanisms. Companies that fail to keep up with these innovations risk losing their competitive edge.
    - **Market Saturation:** With numerous players offering similar products, the market becomes saturated, making it difficult for new entrants to establish themselves and for existing companies to grow.
2. **International Competition:**
    - **Regulatory Compliance:** Competing with international players requires Indian companies to meet stringent regulatory standards, which can be costly and time-consuming.
    - **Brand Recognition and Trust:** International companies often have established brand recognition and trust, especially in regulated markets like the U.S. and Europe. Indian companies must work harder to build a similar reputation.
    - **Technological Advancements:** International competitors often have access to advanced technologies and significant R&D budgets, enabling

them to develop innovative products and maintain a competitive advantage.

Case Study: Strategies Used by a Leading Indian Pharma Company to Stay Competitive

Company: Dr. Reddy's Laboratories

Dr. Reddy's Laboratories is a prime example of an Indian pharmaceutical company that has successfully navigated the competitive landscape through strategic initiatives.

1. **Focus on R&D and Innovation:**
   - Dr. Reddy's invests heavily in research and development to create differentiated products. The company focuses on developing complex generics and biosimilars, which require advanced technological capabilities and offer higher margins compared to standard generics.
   - The company has established multiple R&D centers globally, allowing it to leverage diverse expertise and stay ahead in innovation.
2. **Global Expansion:**
   - To mitigate the risks associated with the highly competitive domestic market, Dr. Reddy's has expanded its presence internationally. The company has established a strong foothold in the U.S., Europe, and emerging markets.
   - This global expansion strategy not only diversifies revenue streams but also reduces dependence on any single market.
3. **Strategic Partnerships and Acquisitions:**
   - Dr. Reddy's has formed strategic partnerships and made acquisitions to enhance its product portfolio and market reach. For instance, the acquisition of Betapharm in Germany allowed the company to strengthen its presence in the European market.

- Collaborations with global pharma companies enable Dr. Reddy's to access new technologies and market opportunities.

4. **Operational Excellence:**
    - The company focuses on operational efficiency to maintain cost competitiveness. Dr. Reddy's has implemented lean manufacturing practices and optimized its supply chain to reduce costs and improve margins.
    - Continuous improvement initiatives ensure that the company remains agile and responsive to market changes.
5. **Regulatory Compliance:**
    - Dr. Reddy's places a strong emphasis on regulatory compliance to ensure its products meet international quality standards. This commitment helps build trust with regulators and consumers alike.
    - The company regularly undergoes audits and inspections to maintain compliance and address any issues proactively.

Outcomes

These strategies have enabled Dr. Reddy's Laboratories to remain competitive in the dynamic pharmaceutical market. The company's focus on innovation, global expansion, strategic partnerships, operational excellence, and regulatory compliance has not only strengthened its market position but also enhanced its reputation as a reliable and innovative player in the global pharmaceutical industry. This case underscores the importance of a multifaceted approach to navigating market competition effectively.

Public Perception Issues

Examination of Public Trust and Perception Issues

Public perception and trust are critical factors influencing the success and reputation of the pharmaceutical industry. In India, the pharmaceutical sector faces several challenges regarding public perception due to factors such as past scandals, instances of drug contamination, and concerns about the quality and affordability of medications. Trust issues can arise from various sources:

1. **Drug Quality and Safety:** Concerns about the quality and safety of drugs produced by Indian pharmaceutical companies can erode public trust. High-profile incidents involving substandard or counterfeit drugs contribute significantly to these concerns.
2. **Transparency and Ethical Practices:** The lack of transparency in clinical trials, drug approval processes, and pricing strategies can lead to skepticism and distrust among the public. Ethical lapses, such as bribery or unethical marketing practices, further exacerbate the issue.
3. **Accessibility and Affordability:** While the Indian pharmaceutical industry is known for producing affordable generic drugs, any perception of price gouging or lack of access to essential medications can negatively impact public trust.
4. **Misinformation:** In the digital age, misinformation about drugs and vaccines can spread rapidly, influencing public perception. Rumors and false information about the side effects, efficacy, and safety of drugs can lead to public fear and mistrust.

Impact of Negative Publicity and Misinformation on the Industry

Negative publicity and misinformation can have severe repercussions for pharmaceutical companies:

1. **Reputation Damage:** Negative publicity can significantly damage a company's reputation. It can lead to a loss of consumer confidence and trust, which are difficult to rebuild. For instance, if a company is implicated in a drug contamination scandal, it can suffer long-lasting reputational damage.
2. **Financial Losses:** Public mistrust can result in decreased sales and revenue. When consumers lose confidence in a company's products, they may turn to competitors, impacting the company's market share and profitability.
3. **Regulatory Scrutiny:** Negative publicity often attracts increased regulatory scrutiny. Companies may face more frequent inspections, stricter regulations, and even penalties, which can further strain their resources.
4. **Litigation Risks:** Misinformation and negative publicity can lead to legal challenges. Consumers affected by substandard or harmful drugs may file lawsuits, leading to significant legal costs and potential settlements.

Case Study: A Crisis Management Situation Handled by an Indian Pharmaceutical Company

Company: Ranbaxy Laboratories

Crisis: Ranbaxy Laboratories faced a significant crisis in 2008 when the U.S. Food and Drug Administration (FDA) banned the import of over 30 drugs manufactured by the company due to quality concerns and data falsification. This incident attracted widespread negative publicity and severely damaged the company's reputation.

Response and Strategies:

1. **Immediate Action:** Ranbaxy immediately acknowledged the issue and initiated corrective actions. The company cooperated fully with regulatory authorities to address the concerns raised by the FDA. This included halting production at affected plants and undertaking a thorough review of their quality control processes.

2. **Transparency and Communication:** Ranbaxy adopted a transparent approach by keeping stakeholders, including regulators, healthcare providers, and the public, informed about the steps being taken to rectify the situation. Regular updates helped in rebuilding trust and demonstrating the company's commitment to quality and safety.
3. **Quality Improvement Initiatives:** The company invested heavily in upgrading its manufacturing facilities and quality control systems. This included hiring international experts to oversee the improvements and implementing stringent quality assurance measures.
4. **Regaining Compliance:** Ranbaxy worked diligently to regain regulatory compliance. The company underwent multiple FDA inspections and audits to ensure that the necessary improvements were made. By demonstrating compliance with international standards, Ranbaxy aimed to restore its credibility.
5. **Corporate Governance and Ethics:** The crisis prompted Ranbaxy to strengthen its corporate governance and ethical practices. The company emphasized the importance of ethical behavior and integrity among its employees and management.

Outcomes:

While the crisis had a significant short-term impact on Ranbaxy's reputation and finances, the company's proactive measures eventually helped it regain regulatory approval and restore some level of trust among stakeholders. However, the long-term damage to its brand was profound, underscoring the critical importance of maintaining high ethical standards and transparency in the pharmaceutical industry.

This case study highlights the importance of effective crisis management and the need for pharmaceutical companies to adopt robust ethical practices to maintain public trust and navigate the challenges posed by negative publicity and misinformation.

Lessons Learned from Leaders' Experiences

There are many lessons that we can learn from our previous leaders' experiences. Let's have a look at these lessons one by one:

1. Adaptive Leadership

Importance of Adaptability in Pharmaceutical Leadership

Adaptability is a cornerstone of effective leadership in the pharmaceutical industry, driven by the sector's inherent complexities, rapid advancements, and regulatory demands. Leaders who exhibit adaptability possess the ability to respond strategically to evolving challenges, capitalize on emerging opportunities, and steer their organizations through turbulent times while maintaining a focus on innovation, compliance, and sustainable growth.

Navigating Regulatory Dynamics:

Pharmaceutical companies operate within a highly regulated environment, subject to stringent national and international standards that continually evolve. Leaders must navigate complex regulatory landscapes, which include drug approval processes, manufacturing standards, clinical trials regulations, and pharmacovigilance requirements. The ability to adapt to regulatory changes and anticipate future compliance demands is crucial for maintaining operational continuity and market competitiveness.

Responding to Technological Advancements:

Advancements in technology, such as biotechnology, artificial intelligence (AI), and digital health solutions, are revolutionizing the pharmaceutical industry. Adaptive leaders embrace these innovations, integrating them into research, development, manufacturing, and commercialization processes. They leverage technological advancements to enhance product efficacy, optimize supply chain management, improve patient outcomes, and differentiate their offerings in a competitive market.

Addressing Market Dynamics:

The pharmaceutical market is dynamic and influenced by factors such as healthcare reforms, pricing pressures, patent expirations, and shifting consumer preferences. Adaptive leaders monitor market trends, anticipate changes in demand, and adjust business strategies accordingly. They may pivot towards specialty medicines, biosimilars, personalized medicine, or digital therapeutics based on market opportunities and patient needs, ensuring sustained revenue growth and market relevance.

Crisis Management and Resilience:

Effective crisis management requires adaptive leadership. Pharmaceutical companies face crises ranging from product recalls and regulatory sanctions to global health emergencies. Adaptive leaders demonstrate resilience, swiftly implementing crisis response plans, mitigating risks, safeguarding patient safety, and preserving stakeholder trust. They communicate transparently, collaborate with regulatory authorities, and uphold ethical standards during crises, reinforcing organizational resilience and long-term viability.

Fostering Innovation:

Innovation is fundamental to pharmaceutical leadership, driving scientific breakthroughs, therapeutic advancements, and competitive differentiation. Adaptive leaders foster a culture of innovation by encouraging interdisciplinary collaboration, empowering research and development teams, and investing in cutting-edge technologies and partnerships. They embrace disruptive innovations that challenge traditional paradigms, such as gene therapies, precision medicine, and digital health solutions, positioning their organizations as pioneers in the evolving healthcare landscape.

Adaptability is not merely a reactive trait but a proactive strategy that enables pharmaceutical leaders to navigate uncertainties, capitalize on opportunities, and drive sustainable growth. By fostering adaptability within their organizations, leaders cultivate resilience, innovation, and agility, positioning their companies to thrive in an increasingly complex and competitive global pharmaceutical industry.

2. Innovative Problem Solving

Innovation plays a pivotal role in the pharmaceutical industry by driving solutions to complex challenges, ranging from drug discovery and development to manufacturing, distribution, and patient care. Here's an exploration of how innovation contributes to addressing industry challenges:

Role of Innovation in Addressing Industry Challenges

1. Drug Discovery and Development:

Innovation in drug discovery is essential for identifying novel compounds that target diseases more effectively with fewer side effects. Traditional approaches to drug discovery have evolved with technological advancements like high-throughput screening, computational modeling, and genomic analysis. These innovations accelerate the identification and validation of drug targets, streamlining the development process and reducing time-to-market for new therapies.

2. Biopharmaceuticals and Biotechnology:

The rise of biopharmaceuticals, including biologics, vaccines, and cell therapies, represents a significant innovation in addressing previously unmet medical needs. Biotechnology enables the production of complex molecules and personalized medicines, offering targeted treatments for conditions like cancer, autoimmune disorders, and rare diseases. Innovations in bioprocessing techniques, such as continuous manufacturing and single-use technologies, enhance production efficiency and scalability, meeting global demand while ensuring product quality and safety.

3. Precision Medicine and Personalized Therapies:

Advancements in genomics, biomarker identification, and data analytics have facilitated the development of precision medicine approaches. These innovations allow healthcare providers to tailor treatment strategies based on a patient's genetic profile, disease characteristics, and lifestyle factors. Precision medicine not only improves treatment outcomes but also minimizes adverse effects, enhancing patient safety and satisfaction.

4. Digital Health and Healthcare Technologies:

Digital health innovations, including telemedicine, wearable devices, health apps, and AI-driven diagnostics, are revolutionizing healthcare delivery and patient management. These technologies facilitate remote monitoring, real-time data analysis, and personalized health insights, empowering patients and healthcare providers alike. In the pharmaceutical industry, digital health solutions streamline clinical trials, improve medication adherence, and enable predictive analytics for drug efficacy and safety.

5. Supply Chain Optimization:

Innovation in supply chain management is crucial for ensuring the efficient distribution and delivery of pharmaceutical products globally. Technologies such as blockchain, IoT (Internet of Things), and predictive analytics optimize inventory management, reduce supply chain disruptions, and enhance transparency and traceability. These innovations bolster supply chain resilience, mitigate risks, and improve access to essential medicines, particularly in remote and underserved regions.

6. Regulatory Compliance and Pharmacovigilance:

Innovations in regulatory compliance and pharmacovigilance are essential for maintaining product quality, safety, and efficacy throughout the pharmaceutical lifecycle. Automated reporting systems, AI-driven surveillance tools, and real-world evidence platforms enhance regulatory compliance monitoring and adverse event detection. These innovations ensure timely regulatory submissions, expedite approvals, and support post-market surveillance, fostering continuous improvement in patient care and public health.

In conclusion, innovation serves as a catalyst for overcoming industry challenges in the pharmaceutical sector. By fostering a culture of innovation and embracing technological advancements, pharmaceutical companies can accelerate drug development, enhance treatment efficacy and safety, optimize supply chain operations, comply with regulatory requirements, and ultimately improve patient outcomes. As the industry continues to evolve, ongoing investment in innovative problem-solving will be crucial for addressing emerging health threats, meeting evolving patient needs, and driving sustainable growth in global healthcare.

3. Strategic Partnerships and Collaboration

Strategic partnerships and collaborations play a crucial role in the pharmaceutical industry, offering numerous benefits that contribute to organizational growth, innovation, and competitive advantage. Here's an exploration of the key benefits:

Benefits of Forming Strategic Partnerships and Collaborations

1. Access to Complementary Expertise and Resources:

One of the primary advantages of strategic partnerships is access to complementary expertise and resources that may not be available internally. Pharmaceutical companies often collaborate with academic institutions, research organizations, biotechnology firms, and technology companies to leverage specialized knowledge, advanced technologies, and intellectual property. These collaborations accelerate research and development (R&D) efforts, facilitate access to novel technologies, and enhance capabilities in areas such as drug discovery, bioprocessing, and clinical trials.

2. Shared Risk and Cost Burden:

Collaborations allow pharmaceutical companies to share the risks and costs associated with R&D, clinical development, and commercialization activities. Developing new drugs is capital-intensive and fraught with uncertainties, including regulatory challenges, market acceptance, and clinical trial outcomes. By pooling resources and expertise through partnerships, companies can mitigate financial risks, optimize resource allocation, and achieve economies of scale. This shared burden enables faster progress from discovery to market, reducing time-to-market for new therapies.

3. Enhanced Innovation and Product Development:

Strategic alliances foster innovation by facilitating cross-disciplinary collaboration and knowledge exchange. Joint research initiatives and co-development agreements enable pharmaceutical companies to combine scientific insights, technologies, and resources to innovate and address unmet medical needs. For example, partnerships between pharmaceutical and biotechnology firms often result in the discovery of breakthrough therapies, including biologics, gene therapies, and personalized medicines. These innovations differentiate companies in competitive markets and enhance their product portfolios.

4. Market Expansion and Access to New Markets:

Partnerships provide opportunities for market expansion by accessing new geographic regions, therapeutic areas, or patient populations. Collaborations with local pharmaceutical companies or distributors facilitate market entry into emerging markets with diverse regulatory landscapes and healthcare infrastructures. Additionally, strategic alliances with global partners enable pharmaceutical firms to navigate international markets, comply with local regulations, and adapt commercial strategies to local preferences and healthcare practices.

5. Accelerated Commercialization and Scale-Up:

Collaborations accelerate the commercialization and scale-up of pharmaceutical products by leveraging partners' established market presence, distribution networks, and sales capabilities. Partnering with contract manufacturing organizations (CMOs) or contract research organizations (CROs) facilitates efficient production, scale-up, and commercial launch of new drugs. This approach minimizes infrastructure investments, reduces time-to-market, and optimizes supply chain logistics, ensuring timely access to medications for patients worldwide.

6. Regulatory and Compliance Advantages:

Strategic partnerships can provide regulatory and compliance advantages, particularly in navigating complex regulatory environments and achieving regulatory approvals. Collaborations with partners experienced in regulatory affairs enhance companies' understanding of local regulations, streamline regulatory submissions, and expedite approvals for clinical trials and marketing authorizations. This proactive approach minimizes compliance risks, ensures adherence to regulatory standards, and maintains product quality and safety throughout the lifecycle.

Strategic partnerships and collaborations are integral to the success of pharmaceutical companies, offering a multitude of benefits that drive innovation, mitigate risks, accelerate market entry, and enhance competitiveness. By fostering strategic alliances with diverse partners, pharmaceutical firms can harness complementary expertise, share costs and risks, accelerate innovation, expand market reach, and achieve regulatory compliance efficiently. As the pharmaceutical landscape continues to evolve, strategic partnerships will remain essential for navigating industry challenges, fostering growth, and ultimately delivering innovative healthcare solutions to patients globally.

Strategies for Navigating Challenges with Resilience and Innovation

Building a Resilient Organizational Culture

Building resilience and fostering innovation are critical strategies for pharmaceutical companies to navigate challenges effectively in a rapidly evolving industry landscape. Here's an exploration of strategies focusing on building a resilient organizational culture:

Importance of Fostering a Resilient and Adaptable Company Culture

1. Navigating Uncertainty and Change:

In the pharmaceutical industry, uncertainty and change are constant. Factors such as regulatory shifts, market dynamics, technological advancements, and global health crises like pandemics can significantly impact operations and strategic planning. A resilient organizational culture equips teams and leaders with the mindset and capabilities to adapt swiftly to these changes. It fosters agility, proactive decision-making, and the ability to pivot strategies in response to external disruptions or internal challenges.

2. Enhancing Employee Engagement and Well-being:

Resilient organizations prioritize employee engagement and well-being, recognizing that motivated and supported employees are more equipped to handle stress and uncertainty. Techniques for building resilience within teams include providing clear communication, fostering trust, offering professional development opportunities, and promoting a healthy work-life balance. Employee support programs, such as mental health initiatives, leadership training, and resilience workshops, equip individuals with coping mechanisms and skills to manage stress effectively.

3. Promoting Innovation and Creativity:

A resilient culture encourages innovation and creativity by fostering an environment where employees feel safe to experiment, take calculated risks, and propose novel solutions. Leaders play a crucial role in promoting a culture of innovation by encouraging idea-sharing, rewarding entrepreneurial thinking, and providing resources for R&D and new product development. Cross-functional collaboration and diversity of thought further stimulate innovation, enabling teams to generate disruptive ideas and solutions to industry challenges.

4. Learning from Adversity and Failure:

Resilient organizations view adversity and failure as opportunities for growth and learning rather than setbacks. They cultivate a mindset that embraces mistakes as valuable learning experiences, encouraging continuous improvement and adaptation. Post-mortem analyses of challenges or failures help identify root causes, refine strategies, and implement corrective actions to prevent recurrence. This iterative approach promotes resilience by building organizational knowledge and adaptive capacity over time.

5. Strategic Risk Management:

Resilient organizations prioritize strategic risk management to anticipate and mitigate potential threats. This involves conducting thorough risk assessments, scenario planning, and developing contingency plans to address various risk scenarios. By proactively identifying risks and implementing mitigation strategies, companies can minimize disruptions to operations, protect their reputation, and maintain stakeholder trust during challenging times.

Techniques for Building Resilience Within Teams and Organizations

1. Leadership Commitment and Role Modeling:

Effective leadership is foundational to building resilience within teams and organizations. Leaders should demonstrate resilience in their decision-making, communication, and response to adversity. By modeling resilience, leaders inspire confidence and trust among employees, motivating them to adopt similar behaviors and attitudes.

2. Cultivating a Supportive Environment:

Creating a supportive work environment is essential for building resilience. This includes promoting open communication, fostering trust and psychological safety, and providing opportunities for feedback and collaboration. Team-building activities, regular check-ins, and mentorship programs enhance camaraderie and solidarity among team members, fostering a sense of collective resilience.

3. Continuous Learning and Adaptation:

Resilient organizations prioritize continuous learning and adaptation to stay ahead of industry trends and challenges. This involves investing in employee training and development, staying abreast of technological advancements, and encouraging cross-functional learning. Learning from past experiences and applying insights to future strategies enables teams to anticipate change, innovate proactively, and adapt quickly to new circumstances.

4. Flexibility and Agility in Operations:

Maintaining flexibility and agility in operational processes enables organizations to respond promptly to market shifts and customer needs. Agile methodologies, such as iterative project management and rapid prototyping, facilitate quick adjustments to strategies based on feedback and changing market conditions. Cross-functional teams empowered to make decentralized decisions further enhance operational agility and responsiveness.

5. Promoting a Culture of Resilience and Innovation:

Building resilience requires a cultural shift where resilience and innovation are embedded in the organization's values, norms, and practices. Celebrating successes, recognizing resilience in action, and acknowledging innovative contributions reinforce desired behaviors. Regular communication about the importance of resilience and innovation reinforces their significance and encourages employees to embrace these principles in their daily work.

Building a resilient organizational culture in the pharmaceutical industry is essential for navigating challenges with agility, fostering innovation, and sustaining long-term success. By prioritizing employee well-being, promoting innovation, learning from adversity, and adopting strategic risk management practices, pharmaceutical companies can enhance their adaptive capacity and effectively respond to the dynamic demands of the industry. This resilient mindset not only ensures operational continuity but also positions organizations to seize opportunities for growth and leadership in an evolving healthcare landscape.

Investing in Research and Development

Research and Development (R&D) plays a pivotal role in the pharmaceutical industry, particularly in overcoming market dynamics and regulatory challenges. Here's an exploration of its significance and strategies for enhancing R&D capabilities and innovation:

Role of R&D in Overcoming Market and Regulatory Challenges

1. Innovation and New Product Development:

R&D is the primary engine for innovation in the pharmaceutical sector. It drives the discovery and development of new medicines, therapies, and technologies that address unmet medical needs and improve patient outcomes. In the face of market competition, R&D enables companies to differentiate themselves by introducing novel treatments that offer superior efficacy, safety profiles, or patient convenience compared to existing therapies. Moreover, innovative products can command premium pricing and gain market share, enhancing profitability and sustainability in a competitive landscape.

2. Navigating Regulatory Requirements:

Pharmaceutical companies must navigate stringent regulatory frameworks imposed by national health authorities (like the CDSCO in India) and international bodies (such as the FDA in the United States or EMA in Europe). R&D plays a crucial role in ensuring compliance with regulatory standards throughout the drug development lifecycle. This includes conducting preclinical studies, clinical trials, and post-marketing surveillance to demonstrate safety, efficacy, and quality of pharmaceutical products. By investing in robust R&D processes and adhering to regulatory guidelines, companies mitigate risks of regulatory non-compliance, expedite market approvals, and maintain public trust.

3. Adapting to Market Dynamics:

Market dynamics in the pharmaceutical industry are influenced by factors such as changing healthcare policies, evolving treatment paradigms, and shifts in patient demographics. R&D enables companies to anticipate and respond to these dynamics by developing innovative therapies aligned with emerging healthcare trends. For example, advancements in precision medicine, biotechnology, and digital health are reshaping R&D priorities towards personalized therapies and integrated healthcare solutions. By investing in adaptive R&D strategies, companies can capitalize on market opportunities, expand therapeutic portfolios, and sustain competitiveness in dynamic market environments.

Strategies for Enhancing R&D Capabilities and Innovation

1. Cross-functional Collaboration:

Effective R&D requires collaboration across disciplines including biomedical sciences, clinical research, regulatory affairs, and commercialization.

Cross-functional teams facilitate knowledge-sharing, synergy in decision-making, and alignment of R&D goals with business objectives. Establishing clear communication channels and fostering a culture of interdisciplinary collaboration enhances efficiency, accelerates innovation cycles, and facilitates seamless progression from discovery to commercialization.

2. Investment in Cutting-edge Technologies:

Technological advancements such as artificial intelligence (AI), machine learning, high-throughput screening, and genomic sequencing are revolutionizing R&D capabilities in the pharmaceutical industry. By leveraging these technologies, companies enhance predictive modeling, accelerate drug discovery processes, optimize clinical trial design, and personalize treatment approaches. Investing in state-of-the-art infrastructure and partnering with technology providers enable pharmaceutical firms to stay at the forefront of scientific innovation and deliver transformative healthcare solutions.

3. Global Partnerships and Collaborations:

Collaborations with academic institutions, research organizations, biotech startups, and contract research organizations (CROs) expand R&D capabilities by accessing diverse expertise, resources, and research networks. Strategic alliances facilitate knowledge exchange, joint funding of R&D projects, and sharing of intellectual property. Furthermore, international collaborations enhance access to global markets, regulatory insights, and patient populations for clinical trials, accelerating the pace of innovation and enhancing competitive advantage.

4. Agile R&D Management Practices:

Adopting agile methodologies in R&D management promotes flexibility, responsiveness, and iterative development cycles. Agile practices enable rapid prototyping, continuous feedback loops, and adaptive decision-making based on real-time data and market insights. By embracing agile principles, pharmaceutical companies streamline R&D operations, reduce time-to-market for new therapies, and effectively address evolving market demands and regulatory requirements.

5. Risk Management and Compliance:

Proactive risk management is integral to successful R&D programs. Companies must assess and mitigate risks associated with clinical trial conduct, regulatory submissions, intellectual property protection, and market acceptance. Implementing robust quality management systems, adhering to ethical standards, and conducting rigorous due diligence in partnership selection ensure compliance with regulatory requirements and safeguard patient safety and trust.

Investing in R&D is essential for pharmaceutical companies to innovate, navigate regulatory complexities, and maintain competitiveness in the global marketplace. By prioritizing strategic investments in interdisciplinary collaboration, cutting-edge technologies, global partnerships, agile management practices, and risk management frameworks, companies enhance their R&D capabilities, accelerate innovation cycles, and deliver transformative healthcare solutions that address critical unmet medical needs. These strategies not only drive business growth and profitability but also contribute to advancing public health outcomes and shaping the future of healthcare innovation.

Leveraging Technology and Digital Transformation

Digital transformation is revolutionizing the pharmaceutical industry, offering profound impacts across various facets of operations, innovation, and patient care:

1. **Drug Discovery and Development:** Digital technologies such as artificial intelligence (AI), machine learning, and big data analytics are transforming the drug discovery process. These tools analyze vast amounts of data from genomic sequencing, molecular modeling, and clinical trials to identify potential drug targets, predict drug interactions, and optimize therapeutic efficacy. AI-powered algorithms accelerate screening of compound libraries, enabling researchers to prioritize promising candidates and reduce time and costs associated with preclinical research.
2. **Clinical Trials and Patient Recruitment:** Digital platforms streamline clinical trial management by automating patient recruitment, enrollment, and monitoring processes. Telemedicine, wearable devices, and remote patient monitoring facilitate real-time data collection, enhancing trial efficiency, patient adherence, and data accuracy. Digital tools also support virtual trials, enabling broader patient participation and reducing geographical barriers, thereby accelerating trial timelines and enhancing diversity in study populations.
3. **Precision Medicine and Personalized Healthcare:** Digital technologies enable personalized treatment approaches based on individual patient data, including genetic profiles, biomarkers, and lifestyle factors. Computational modeling and predictive analytics enhance disease stratification, treatment selection, and therapeutic outcomes by tailoring interventions to patient-specific characteristics. Virtual care platforms and digital therapeutics deliver personalized interventions, patient education, and remote monitoring to optimize treatment adherence and health outcomes.

4. **Supply Chain Management and Operational Efficiency:** Digital solutions improve supply chain transparency, inventory management, and logistics in pharmaceutical manufacturing and distribution. Blockchain technology enhances traceability and authentication of pharmaceutical products, reducing counterfeit drugs and ensuring compliance with regulatory requirements. IoT-enabled sensors monitor environmental conditions during storage and transportation, maintaining product quality and safety while minimizing waste and supply chain disruptions.
5. **Patient Engagement and Healthcare Delivery:** Digital platforms empower patients with access to health information, self-management tools, and telehealth services, promoting active participation in their care journey. Mobile apps, patient portals, and virtual consultations enable remote access to healthcare providers, enhancing convenience, patient satisfaction, and adherence to treatment regimens. Patient-generated data and digital health records facilitate care coordination, personalized health planning, and continuous monitoring, fostering proactive disease management and improving health outcomes.

In essence, digital transformation in the pharmaceutical industry accelerates innovation, enhances operational efficiencies, and improves patient-centric care delivery. By leveraging advanced technologies, pharmaceutical companies optimize R&D processes, streamline clinical operations, and transform healthcare delivery models to meet evolving market demands and deliver value-driven solutions that address global health challenges.

In the dynamic landscape of the pharmaceutical industry, resilience and innovation are not just advantageous but essential for navigating challenges and seizing opportunities. Resilience enables organizations to withstand setbacks, adapt to regulatory changes, and overcome market uncertainties. It fosters an agile response to disruptions, ensuring continuity in operations and maintaining stakeholder trust amidst challenges like regulatory complexities, market competition, and public perception issues.

In parallel, innovation drives progress by fostering creativity, problem-solving, and the development of novel solutions. Whether through advancements in R&D, digital transformation, or strategic collaborations, innovative approaches empower pharmaceutical companies to stay ahead of the curve. They enable quicker adaptation to changing market dynamics, facilitate breakthroughs in treatment modalities, and enhance operational efficiencies.

As the industry continues to evolve, embracing resilience and innovation as core strategies is paramount. Leaders must foster a culture that values continuous learning, encourages experimentation, and embraces transformative technologies. By doing so, they not only navigate current challenges effectively but also position their organizations to lead in shaping the future of healthcare through groundbreaking discoveries and sustainable growth.

Chapter 8
Visionary Leadership for Sustainable Success

The pharmaceutical industry in India is experiencing rapid transformation, driven by technological advancements, regulatory reforms, and shifting global trends. In this dynamic environment, leadership plays a pivotal role in navigating complexities and seizing opportunities. Visionary leaders are crucial for driving innovation, ensuring compliance with evolving regulations, and maintaining a competitive edge in the global market. This chapter delves into the evolving role of leadership within this context, emphasizing the need for adaptability and forward-thinking strategies.

Technological advancements such as artificial intelligence, big data analytics, and automation are revolutionizing how pharmaceutical companies operate, from research and development to manufacturing and distribution. Regulatory reforms, both domestic and international, require leaders to stay abreast of new laws and guidelines to ensure compliance and mitigate risks. Additionally, global trends like increasing collaborations, outsourcing, and the push for sustainability are reshaping the industry landscape. Leaders must be adept at understanding and integrating these trends to achieve sustainable success.

The purpose of this chapter is to provide a comprehensive understanding of visionary leadership in the Indian pharmaceutical industry, focusing on the principles and practices that enable leaders to drive sustainable success. We will explore how leaders can leverage technological advancements, adapt to regulatory changes, and respond to global trends effectively.

Evolving Leadership in the Indian Pharmaceutical Landscape

Technological Advancements

The pharmaceutical industry is undergoing a significant transformation fueled by technological advancements. These innovations are reshaping various aspects of the industry, from drug discovery and development to manufacturing, distribution, and patient engagement. Key technological advancements include:

1. **Artificial Intelligence (AI) and Machine Learning (ML)**:
   AI and ML are revolutionizing drug discovery and development by enabling the analysis of vast datasets to identify potential drug candidates more quickly and accurately. These technologies can predict molecular behavior, optimize clinical trial design, and enhance personalized medicine approaches.
2. **Big Data and Analytics**:
   Big data analytics allow pharmaceutical companies to harness and interpret massive amounts of data generated from clinical trials, patient records, and real-world evidence. This enables better decision-making, improved patient outcomes, and more efficient resource allocation.
3. **Automation and Robotics**:
   Automation and robotics are streamlining manufacturing processes, increasing efficiency, and reducing human error. Automated systems can handle repetitive tasks, ensuring consistent product quality and freeing up human resources for more complex activities.
4. **Blockchain Technology**:
   Blockchain technology enhances transparency and traceability in the pharmaceutical supply chain. It helps in combating counterfeit drugs, ensuring data integrity, and improving regulatory compliance by providing an immutable ledger of transactions.

5. **Internet of Things (IoT)**:
   IoT devices are being used for remote patient monitoring, enhancing adherence to treatment plans, and collecting real-time health data. This technology is particularly beneficial in managing chronic diseases and improving patient outcomes.
6. **Telemedicine and Digital Health**:

   The rise of telemedicine and digital health platforms has transformed patient care, making healthcare services more accessible and convenient. These platforms facilitate remote consultations, follow-ups, and real-time patient monitoring.

Discussion on How Leaders Can Leverage Technology to Drive Innovation and Efficiency

For leaders in the Indian pharmaceutical industry, leveraging these technological advancements is essential for driving innovation and efficiency. Here are key strategies to effectively harness these technologies:

1. **Embracing a Digital Transformation Mindset**:

   Leaders must champion a culture of digital transformation within their organizations. This involves fostering an environment where technological adoption is encouraged and supported at all levels. Investing in digital literacy and training programs for employees can help build a tech-savvy workforce capable of leveraging new tools and systems.
2. **Investing in R&D and Innovation**:
   Continuous investment in research and development (R&D) is crucial for staying at the forefront of technological advancements. Leaders should allocate resources to explore emerging technologies and their applications in drug discovery, development, and manufacturing. Collaborating with tech startups, research institutions, and industry partners can also spur innovation.

3. **Implementing Data-Driven Decision Making**: Utilizing big data and analytics can provide valuable insights into market trends, patient needs, and operational efficiencies. Leaders should prioritize data-driven decision-making processes, integrating analytics into strategic planning and day-to-day operations. This approach can enhance product development, optimize supply chain management, and improve patient outcomes.
4. **Enhancing Operational Efficiency through Automation**: Automation and robotics can significantly improve operational efficiency by reducing manual errors, increasing production speed, and ensuring consistent product quality. Leaders should identify areas where automation can be implemented, such as manufacturing, packaging, and quality control, to streamline processes and reduce costs.
5. **Ensuring Robust Cybersecurity Measures**: As the industry becomes more digitized, protecting sensitive data from cyber threats is paramount. Leaders must invest in robust cybersecurity measures to safeguard patient information, intellectual property, and operational data. This includes implementing encryption, secure access controls, and regular security audits.
6. **Fostering Collaboration and Partnerships**: Collaborating with technology providers, academic institutions, and other industry players can accelerate the adoption of new technologies. Leaders should actively seek partnerships that can provide access to cutting-edge technologies, expertise, and resources. Collaborative efforts can lead to the co-creation of innovative solutions and enhance overall industry standards.
7. **Regulatory Compliance and Ethical Considerations**: While adopting new technologies, leaders must ensure compliance with regulatory requirements and uphold ethical standards. This involves staying updated with evolving regulations, implementing robust compliance frameworks, and conducting ethical reviews of new technological applications.

By strategically leveraging technological advancements, leaders in the Indian pharmaceutical industry can drive innovation, improve operational efficiency, and enhance patient care. Embracing a forward-thinking approach and investing in technology will position companies to thrive in an increasingly competitive and dynamic landscape.

Regulatory Reforms

Examination of Recent and Upcoming Regulatory Reforms in India

The pharmaceutical industry operates under regulatory framework designed to ensure the safety, efficacy, and quality of medicines. Recent and upcoming regulatory reforms are aimed at strengthening this framework, enhancing compliance, and fostering innovation. Key regulatory reforms include:

1. **The New Drugs and Clinical Trials Rules, 2019**:

   This comprehensive regulatory overhaul aims to streamline the approval process for new drugs and clinical trials. It introduces provisions for accelerated approval of drugs for unmet medical needs and emphasizes patient safety and ethical standards in clinical research.

2. **Amendments to the Drugs and Cosmetics Act**:

   Recent amendments focus on improving the quality control of drugs and cosmetics. These include stricter penalties for manufacturing and selling substandard or spurious products, enhanced surveillance of manufacturing facilities, and better enforcement mechanisms.

3. **Implementation of Pharmacovigilance Programs**:

   Strengthening pharmacovigilance programs to monitor and manage adverse drug reactions is a significant regulatory focus. This involves establishing comprehensive reporting systems and ensuring that pharmaceutical companies comply with pharmacovigilance requirements.

4. **Good Manufacturing Practices (GMP) Compliance**:

   The Indian government has been reinforcing GMP guidelines to ensure that pharmaceutical manufacturing processes meet international standards. This includes regular audits and inspections of manufacturing facilities to ensure compliance with quality standards.

5. **E-Governance Initiatives**:

   To improve transparency and efficiency, the Indian regulatory authorities are increasingly adopting digital solutions. Initiatives like the SUGAM portal for online submission and tracking of regulatory applications aim to reduce bureaucratic delays and enhance regulatory oversight.

Strategies for Leaders to Navigate and Adapt to Regulatory Changes

Navigating and adapting to regulatory changes requires strategic planning and proactive measures from leaders in the pharmaceutical industry. Key strategies include:

1. **Staying Informed and Engaged**:

   Leaders must stay abreast of regulatory developments by actively engaging with regulatory authorities, industry associations, and professional networks. Regularly attending conferences, workshops, and training sessions can help keep the organization updated on new regulations and compliance requirements.

2. **Building a Strong Regulatory Affairs Team**:

   Establishing a dedicated regulatory affairs team that understands the intricacies of both domestic and international regulations is crucial. This team should be responsible for monitoring regulatory changes, assessing their impact on the company, and ensuring timely compliance.

3. **Implementing Robust Compliance Systems**:

   Developing and maintaining comprehensive compliance systems is essential to meet regulatory requirements. This includes conducting regular internal audits, implementing standardized operating procedures, and ensuring proper documentation and record-keeping.

4. **Fostering a Culture of Compliance**:

   Leaders should promote a culture of compliance within the organization by emphasizing the importance of adhering to regulatory standards. This involves training employees on regulatory requirements, encouraging ethical practices, and setting clear expectations for compliance.

5. **Leveraging Technology for Compliance**:

   Utilizing digital tools and technologies can enhance compliance efforts. Implementing electronic quality management systems (eQMS), digital audit trails, and automated reporting systems can streamline compliance processes and reduce the risk of non-compliance.

6. **Collaborating with External Experts**:

   Engaging with regulatory consultants, legal advisors, and industry experts can provide valuable insights and guidance on navigating regulatory changes. These collaborations can help identify potential compliance challenges and develop effective strategies to address them.

By adopting these strategies, leaders can effectively navigate regulatory changes, ensure compliance, and position their organizations for sustainable growth in a dynamic regulatory environment.

Cultivating a Visionary Mindset

Steps for Leaders to Develop and Maintain a Visionary Mindset

1. **Continuous Learning**:

   Stay updated with industry trends, technological advancements, and global developments. This involves reading industry journals, attending conferences, and participating in professional development programs. Lifelong learning helps leaders anticipate future changes and adapt accordingly.

2. **Embrace Innovation**:

   Encourage a culture of innovation within the organization. This means not just being open to new ideas but actively seeking them out. Leaders should foster an environment where creativity is valued, and experimentation is encouraged.

3. **Strategic Networking**:

   Build relationships with other industry leaders, regulators, and stakeholders. Networking provides diverse perspectives and insights that can help leaders foresee industry shifts and identify new opportunities.

4. **Scenario Planning**:

   Engage in scenario planning to explore various future possibilities and their potential impacts. This helps leaders prepare for different outcomes and develop flexible strategies that can be adjusted as circumstances change.

5. **Vision Workshops**:

   Conduct workshops that involve key team members in vision-building exercises. This collaborative approach ensures that the vision is shared and supported across the organization, fostering a collective commitment to achieving long-term goals.

6. **Reflection and Adaptation**:

   Regularly reflect on past decisions and outcomes. Understanding what worked, what didn't, and why helps refine future strategies. Leaders should be willing to adapt their vision as new information and insights emerge.

Importance of Foresight and Strategic Thinking in Leadership

1. **Anticipating Changes**:

   Foresight enables leaders to anticipate changes in the market, regulatory environment, and technological landscape. By predicting potential shifts, leaders can proactively adjust their strategies to maintain a competitive edge.

2. **Long-Term Planning**:

Strategic thinking is essential for long-term planning. It allows leaders to set clear, achievable goals that align with the company's vision and mission. This long-term perspective ensures that the organization remains focused on sustainable growth and innovation.

3. **Risk Management**:

Visionary leaders are adept at identifying and mitigating risks. By considering various scenarios and their potential impacts, leaders can develop contingency plans to navigate uncertainties and minimize disruptions.

4. **Driving Innovation**:

A visionary mindset drives innovation by encouraging leaders to think beyond the present and envision future possibilities. This forward-thinking approach inspires creativity and motivates teams to develop groundbreaking solutions that address emerging challenges.

5. **Inspiring and Guiding Teams**:

Visionary leaders inspire their teams by communicating a compelling vision of the future. This inspires employees to work towards shared goals and fosters a sense of purpose and direction within the organization.

6. **Building Resilience**:

Foresight and strategic thinking build organizational resilience by preparing leaders and their teams for potential challenges. This proactive approach ensures that the organization can quickly adapt to changes and continue to thrive in a dynamic environment.

By cultivating a visionary mindset, leaders can navigate the complexities of the pharmaceutical industry, drive innovation, and ensure their organizations remain competitive and sustainable in the long run.

Fostering Innovation and Creativity

Techniques for Fostering a Culture of Innovation within Pharmaceutical Organizations

1. **Encouraging Open Communication**:

   Create an environment where employees feel comfortable sharing ideas and feedback without fear of criticism. Open communication channels facilitate the exchange of innovative ideas and solutions.

2. **Promoting Cross-Functional Collaboration**:

   Encourage collaboration across different departments to bring diverse perspectives and expertise to the table. Cross-functional teams can solve complex problems more creatively than siloed groups.

3. **Allocating Resources for Innovation**:

   Invest in resources such as R&D, technology, and training programs that support innovative projects. Providing the necessary tools and funding shows a commitment to fostering innovation.

4. **Implementing Idea Management Systems**:

   Use idea management platforms to capture, evaluate, and implement ideas from employees. Such systems help track the progress of innovative ideas and ensure they receive the attention they deserve.

5. **Recognizing and Rewarding Innovation**:

   Acknowledge and reward employees who contribute innovative ideas and solutions. Recognition programs and incentives can motivate employees to think creatively and take risks.

Role of Leadership in Encouraging Creativity and Risk-Taking

1. **Leading by Example**:

   Leaders should demonstrate a willingness to explore new ideas and take calculated risks. Their behavior sets the tone for the organization and encourages employees to do the same.

2. **Providing Psychological Safety**:

   Create a culture where employees feel safe to experiment and fail. Understanding that failure is a part of the innovation process reduces the fear of taking risks and promotes a learning environment.

3. **Offering Continuous Learning Opportunities**:

   Provide opportunities for employees to learn new skills and stay updated with industry trends. Training programs, workshops, and seminars can stimulate creative thinking and innovation.

4. **Setting Clear Innovation Goals**:

   Define clear innovation goals and communicate them to the entire organization. Aligning these goals with the company's vision and mission provides direction and purpose to innovation efforts.

Building Resilient Teams

Strategies for Building and Leading Resilient Teams

1. **Hiring for Diversity**:

   Build teams with diverse backgrounds, skills, and perspectives. Diversity fosters creativity, innovation, and adaptability, enabling teams to approach problems from different angles.

2. **Strengthening Team Cohesion**:

   Promote team-building activities and initiatives that strengthen relationships and trust among team members. Strong cohesion enhances collaboration and collective problem-solving abilities.

3. **Encouraging Flexibility and Adaptability**:

   Develop a culture that embraces change and is adaptable to new circumstances. Encourage team members to be flexible in their roles and responsibilities to respond to evolving challenges.

4. **Providing Support and Resources**:

   Ensure teams have access to the necessary resources and support to perform effectively. This includes providing training, tools, and a supportive work environment.

5. **Promoting Work-Life Balance:**

   Encourage a healthy work-life balance to prevent burnout and maintain high levels of productivity and morale. Flexible work arrangements and wellness programs can support this balance.

Importance of Team Cohesion, Diversity, and Adaptability

1. **Enhanced Problem-Solving:**

   Diverse teams bring a range of perspectives and experiences, leading to more innovative and effective solutions. Team cohesion ensures that these diverse perspectives are integrated harmoniously.

2. **Increased Resilience:**

   Teams that are adaptable and cohesive can better navigate challenges and disruptions. Their ability to support each other and work collaboratively under pressure strengthens overall resilience.

3. **Improved Performance:**

   High levels of trust and collaboration within teams lead to improved performance and efficiency. When team members feel valued and supported, they are more motivated and productive.

Ethical Decision-Making and Integrity

Frameworks for Ethical Decision-Making in Leadership

1. **Ethical Decision-Making Models**:

   Utilize established models such as the Utilitarian Approach (maximizing overall good), Rights Approach (respecting and protecting individual rights), and Fairness Approach (treating everyone equally and fairly) to guide decisions.

2. **Stakeholder Analysis**:

   Consider the impact of decisions on all stakeholders, including employees, customers, shareholders, and the community. Balancing the interests of different stakeholders ensures fair and ethical outcomes.

3. **Transparency and Accountability**:

   Maintain transparency in decision-making processes and hold leaders accountable for their actions. Open communication about decisions and their rationales builds trust and credibility.

Importance of Integrity in Maintaining Trust and Credibility

1. **Building Trust with Stakeholders**:

   Integrity fosters trust among stakeholders, which is crucial for long-term success. Trustworthy leaders inspire confidence and loyalty, enhancing relationships with employees, customers, and partners.

2. **Enhancing Company Reputation**:

   Companies known for ethical practices and integrity attract talent, investors, and customers. A strong reputation for integrity differentiates the company in a competitive market.

3. **Ensuring Sustainable Success**:

   Ethical decision-making and integrity contribute to sustainable success by avoiding scandals, legal issues, and reputational damage. Companies that prioritize integrity are better positioned to thrive in the long run.

4. **Promoting a Positive Organizational Culture**:

   Leaders who model ethical behavior set the standard for the entire organization. This promotes a culture of integrity, accountability, and ethical conduct, positively influencing employee behavior and company performance.

Driving Sustainable Success

Sustainability in the Pharmaceutical Industry

The pharmaceutical industry faces several sustainability challenges that necessitate the adoption of innovative and ethical practices. These challenges include environmental impact, resource scarcity, and the need for sustainable supply chains. Despite these challenges, there are significant opportunities for the pharmaceutical industry to drive sustainability:

1. **Green Chemistry**:

   Implementing green chemistry principles in drug manufacturing can reduce the environmental impact by minimizing the use of hazardous substances and energy consumption.

2. **Circular Economy**:
   Adopting circular economy practices, such as recycling and reusing materials, can significantly reduce waste and resource consumption.

3. **Renewable Energy**:

   Investing in renewable energy sources for manufacturing processes can help reduce the industry's carbon footprint and reliance on non-renewable resources.

Role of Leadership in Driving Sustainable Practices and Initiatives

Leadership plays a crucial role in promoting and implementing sustainable practices within the pharmaceutical industry. Visionary leaders who prioritize sustainability can drive significant positive change by setting clear goals, inspiring their teams, and fostering a culture of environmental responsibility.

1. **Setting Clear Sustainability Goals**:

   Leaders must define clear and achievable sustainability goals aligned with the organization's mission and values. These goals should address key sustainability challenges and focus on long-term impact.

2. **Incorporating Sustainability into Corporate Strategy**:

   Integrating sustainability into the core corporate strategy ensures that it becomes a fundamental aspect of business operations rather than an afterthought. This includes embedding sustainability metrics into performance evaluations and decision-making processes.

3. **Fostering a Culture of Sustainability**:

   Leaders should promote a culture where sustainability is valued and prioritized. This involves educating employees about sustainable practices, encouraging eco-friendly initiatives, and recognizing and rewarding contributions to sustainability.

4. **Engaging Stakeholders**:

   Engaging with stakeholders, including suppliers, customers, and communities, is essential for driving sustainability. Leaders must collaborate with stakeholders to develop and implement sustainable practices across the value chain.

5. **Investing in Innovation**:

   Leadership should champion innovation in sustainable technologies and practices. Investing in research and development of sustainable solutions can lead to breakthroughs that reduce environmental impact and improve resource efficiency.

6. **Transparency and Reporting**:

   Maintaining transparency in sustainability efforts through regular reporting builds trust with stakeholders and demonstrates commitment to sustainable practices. Leaders should ensure that sustainability reports are accurate, comprehensive, and accessible.

By prioritizing sustainability and leveraging their influence, leaders in the pharmaceutical industry can drive meaningful change, ensuring long-term success and a positive impact on the environment and society.

Balancing Profitability and Social Responsibility

Balancing profitability with social responsibility is a critical challenge for leaders in the pharmaceutical industry. Effective strategies that harmonize these two objectives can result in sustainable business practices that benefit both the company and society.

1. **Integrating CSR into Core Business Strategy**:

   Corporate Social Responsibility (CSR) should not be viewed as a separate or secondary activity. By integrating CSR into the core business strategy, companies can align their profit motives with societal benefits. This approach ensures that social responsibility is embedded in every aspect of the business, from product development to marketing.

2. **Innovative Product Development**:

   Developing affordable medications for populations can drive both social impact and business growth. By focusing on diseases prevalent in low-income regions and creating cost-effective treatments, pharmaceutical companies can open new markets while fulfilling social responsibilities.

3. **Sustainable Supply Chain Management**:

   Implementing sustainable practices within the supply chain can reduce costs and enhance corporate reputation. For instance, sourcing raw materials ethically and minimizing waste through efficient processes can lower operational costs and appeal to socially conscious consumers and investors.

4. **Partnerships and Collaborations**:

   Collaborating with non-governmental organizations (NGOs), and other stakeholders can amplify the impact of social initiatives. Such partnerships can provide resources, expertise, and networks that help in addressing complex health issues while ensuring business viability.

5. **Employee Engagement**:

   Encouraging employees to participate in social responsibility initiatives can boost morale, enhance skills, and foster a sense of purpose. This engagement can translate into higher productivity and loyalty, positively impacting the company's bottom line.

6. **Transparent Reporting**:

   Maintaining transparency in social responsibility efforts builds trust with stakeholders. Regularly publishing sustainability reports that outline both financial performance and social impact can attract socially responsible investors and customers.

Examples of Successful Initiatives:

1. **GSK's "Africa 2020" Strategy**:

   GlaxoSmithKline (GSK) implemented a strategy focused on increasing access to medicines in Africa by reducing prices and investing in local healthcare infrastructure. This initiative not only expanded GSK's market presence but also significantly improved healthcare access.

2. **Novartis Access Program**:

   Novartis launched a program to provide affordable treatments for chronic diseases in low- and middle-income countries. This initiative balances profitability and social responsibility by leveraging economies of scale to offer lower-priced medicines while reaching a broader patient base.

By adopting these strategies, pharmaceutical companies can achieve a balance between profitability and social responsibility, leading to sustainable business growth and positive societal impact.

Long-Term Vision and Strategic Planning

Long-term vision and strategic planning are fundamental to achieving sustainable success in the pharmaceutical industry. They provide a roadmap for navigating challenges, seizing opportunities, and aligning organizational efforts with broader societal needs and expectations.

Importance of Long-Term Vision:

1. **Guiding Organizational Direction**: A clear long-term vision articulates where the organization aims to be in the future. It serves as a guiding light for decision-making, ensuring that all activities and initiatives are aligned with overarching goals.
2. **Adaptability and Resilience**: In a dynamic and evolving industry like pharmaceuticals, long-term vision enables companies to anticipate changes and adapt proactively. It fosters resilience by preparing the organization to weather short-term disruptions while staying focused on long-term objectives.
3. **Stakeholder Confidence**: Stakeholders, including investors, employees, and customers, value consistency and foresight. A well-defined long-term vision instills confidence by demonstrating that the company has a clear strategy for sustained growth and impact.

Techniques for Setting and Achieving Long-Term Goals:

1. **Environmental Scanning**: Continuously monitor the external environment, including regulatory changes, market trends, and technological advancements. This information helps in identifying opportunities and threats that can influence long-term strategies.

2. **Scenario Planning**: Develop multiple scenarios of possible futures based on different assumptions. This approach helps in preparing for various outcomes and crafting flexible strategies that can adapt to changing circumstances.
3. **Strategic Alignment**: Ensure that long-term goals are aligned with the company's mission, values, and core competencies. This alignment ensures coherence across all levels of the organization and facilitates focused resource allocation.
4. **Key Performance Indicators (KPIs)**: Establish clear KPIs that measure progress toward long-term goals. Regularly review and adjust these metrics to reflect changing priorities and market conditions.
5. **Engage Stakeholders**: Involve key stakeholders in the strategic planning process to gain diverse perspectives and build consensus around long-term objectives. This inclusivity enhances commitment and collective effort toward achieving shared goals.
6. **Continuous Evaluation and Adaptation**: Regularly review progress against long-term goals and be prepared to adapt strategies based on performance feedback and external developments. Flexibility and agility are crucial for staying on course toward long-term success.

By emphasizing long-term vision and strategic planning, pharmaceutical companies can navigate uncertainty, capitalize on opportunities, and achieve sustainable success while maintaining a focus on ethical practices and social responsibility.

In conclusion, the landscape of leadership in the pharmaceutical industry demands a forward-thinking approach that integrates visionary strategies with ethical responsibility and sustainability. As we reflect on the insights gathered throughout this chapter, it becomes clear that leaders must navigate complex challenges such as technological advancements, regulatory reforms, and evolving societal expectations with resilience and innovation.

Firstly, it is imperative for current and aspiring leaders in the pharmaceutical sector to embrace visionary leadership. This entails not only anticipating future trends and challenges but also envisioning opportunities that align business objectives with societal needs. Visionary leaders inspire their teams to innovate, adapt, and drive meaningful change within their organizations and communities.

Secondly, continuous learning and adaptation are critical components of sustainable success. In an industry characterized by rapid advancements and regulatory shifts, leaders must cultivate a culture of lifelong learning among their teams. This involves staying abreast of emerging technologies, industry trends, and best practices in ethical leadership and sustainability. By fostering a learning mindset, leaders empower their organizations to remain agile and responsive to evolving market dynamics.

Lastly, commitment to sustainable success requires a steadfast dedication to ethical practices and corporate social responsibility. Leaders must uphold integrity, transparency, and accountability in all aspects of their operations, from R&D and manufacturing to marketing and distribution. By prioritizing ethical decision-making and social responsibility, pharmaceutical companies can build trust with stakeholders, enhance brand reputation, and contribute positively to global health outcomes.

In essence, visionary and heart-led leadership is not merely about achieving short-term profitability but about laying the groundwork for sustainable growth and positive societal impact. By embracing these principles and taking proactive steps to address industry challenges, leaders can steer their organizations toward a future where innovation, integrity, and resilience define success in the pharmaceutical industry.

Chapter 9
The Lasting Impact of Compassionate Leadership

The pharmaceutical sector faces unique challenges, including regulatory complexities, market competition, and public perception issues. Compassionate leadership, characterized by empathy, integrity, and a genuine concern for the well-being of employees, patients, and communities, is essential for addressing these challenges effectively. By fostering a supportive and inclusive environment, compassionate leaders can enhance organizational resilience, drive ethical innovation, and build strong, trust-based relationships with stakeholders. This leadership style not only improves business outcomes but also contributes to the broader goal of enhancing public health and well-being in India.

Relevance of Compassionate Leadership in the Indian Pharmaceutical Industry

Addressing Challenges with Compassionate Leadership

As we discussed in the book, the Indian pharmaceutical industry faces a complex array of challenges. Compassionate leadership, which emphasizes empathy, ethical decision-making, and a commitment to the well-being of all stakeholders, is particularly well-suited to navigate these challenges.

Compassionate leaders are adept at fostering a culture of openness and trust within their organizations. By prioritizing transparent communication and ethical practices, they can effectively address regulatory complexities. For example, a compassionate leader might implement stringent compliance protocols and invest in training programs to ensure that all employees understand and adhere to regulatory requirements. This proactive approach not only mitigates the risk of non-compliance but also builds a reputation for integrity and reliability.

In the face of intense market competition, compassionate leadership can serve as a differentiator. Leaders who demonstrate genuine concern for their employees' well-being can cultivate a motivated and loyal workforce, which is crucial for maintaining a competitive edge. Moreover, by fostering an inclusive and supportive work environment, compassionate leaders can enhance employee engagement and productivity, leading to innovative solutions and improved organizational performance.

Role in Fostering Innovation and Adaptability

Innovation and adaptability are essential for the long-term success of pharmaceutical companies. Compassionate leadership plays a critical role in fostering these qualities by creating an environment where employees feel valued and empowered to contribute their ideas.

Compassionate leaders encourage open dialogue and collaboration, which are key drivers of innovation. They recognize the importance of diverse perspectives and actively seek input from all levels of the organization. This inclusive approach not only generates a broader range of ideas but also enhances the organization's ability to adapt to changing market conditions and technological advancements.

Furthermore, compassionate leaders are more likely to invest in the professional development of their employees. By providing opportunities for continuous learning and growth, they equip their teams with the skills and knowledge needed to navigate the rapidly evolving pharmaceutical landscape. This commitment to employee development fosters a culture of innovation and adaptability, ensuring that the organization remains competitive in the long run.

Enhancing Patient-Centric Approaches and Improving Public Perception

In the pharmaceutical industry, a patient-centric approach is essential for building trust and ensuring the efficacy of treatments. Compassionate leadership inherently aligns with patient-centricity, as it prioritizes the needs and well-being of patients.

Compassionate leaders advocate for the development of treatments and services that genuinely improve patient outcomes. They ensure that patient feedback is integrated into the decision-making process, leading to more effective and user-friendly products. By putting patients at the center of their strategies, compassionate leaders can enhance patient satisfaction and loyalty, ultimately contributing to better health outcomes.

Moreover, compassionate leadership can significantly improve public perception of pharmaceutical companies. In an industry often criticized for prioritizing profits over patient welfare, leaders who demonstrate empathy and ethical responsibility can rebuild public trust. By transparently addressing issues such as drug pricing and accessibility, compassionate leaders can demonstrate their commitment to social responsibility and ethical practices.

Public trust is further strengthened when compassionate leaders engage with communities and stakeholders. By participating in community outreach programs and collaborating with healthcare providers and policymakers, they can ensure that their companies are seen as partners in improving public health. This positive public perception not only enhances the company's reputation but also fosters a supportive environment for business growth and innovation.

Compassionate leadership is highly relevant in the Indian pharmaceutical industry as it effectively addresses key challenges, fosters innovation and adaptability, and enhances patient-centric approaches and public perception. By prioritizing empathy, ethical practices, and stakeholder well-being, compassionate leaders can drive sustainable success and positive change in the industry.

Future Outlook of the Pharmaceutical Industry and the Role of Compassionate Leadership

Emerging Trends and Future Challenges

The pharmaceutical industry is on the cusp of transformative change driven by technological advancements. Innovations such as artificial intelligence (AI), machine learning (ML), and big data analytics are revolutionizing drug discovery, development, and delivery. AI and ML can analyze vast datasets to identify potential drug candidates more quickly and accurately than traditional methods, reducing the time and cost associated with bringing new treatments to market. Additionally, advancements in genomics and personalized medicine are enabling more targeted and effective therapies, tailored to the unique genetic profiles of individual patients.

Compassionate leadership plays a crucial role in navigating these technological advancements. Leaders who prioritize empathy and ethical considerations ensure that technological innovations are implemented in ways that benefit patients and society. For example, compassionate leaders might advocate for the use of AI in patient care settings to enhance diagnostic accuracy and treatment personalization, while also addressing concerns about data privacy and ethical use of patient information.

Evolving Regulatory Landscapes and Global Market Dynamics

The regulatory environment for pharmaceuticals is becoming increasingly complex and stringent. Regulatory agencies worldwide are implementing more rigorous standards for drug safety, efficacy, and quality. Additionally, the globalization of the pharmaceutical market presents challenges related to compliance with diverse regulatory frameworks across different countries. These evolving regulatory landscapes require pharmaceutical companies to be agile and proactive in their compliance strategies.

Compassionate leadership is essential in this context as well. Compassionate leaders prioritize transparency and ethical conduct, which are key to building trust with regulators and stakeholders. They are committed to maintaining high standards of compliance and quality, recognizing that patient safety and well-being are paramount. By fostering a culture of integrity and accountability, compassionate leaders can navigate regulatory complexities more effectively and maintain positive relationships with regulatory authorities.

Increasing Emphasis on Sustainability and Social Responsibility

Sustainability and social responsibility are becoming central to the future of the pharmaceutical industry. Stakeholders, including patients, healthcare providers, investors, and regulators, are increasingly demanding that pharmaceutical companies operate in environmentally and socially responsible ways. This includes reducing the environmental impact of manufacturing processes, ensuring equitable access to medications, and addressing global health challenges such as antibiotic resistance and pandemics.

Compassionate leadership is critical in advancing sustainability and social responsibility initiatives. Compassionate leaders understand that their companies have a broader responsibility to society and the environment. They champion initiatives that reduce carbon footprints, promote ethical sourcing of raw materials, and support global health initiatives. By aligning business practices with sustainable and socially responsible values, compassionate leaders can build stronger relationships with stakeholders and enhance their company's reputation.

The Role of Compassionate Leadership in Addressing Future Challenges

As the pharmaceutical industry evolves, compassionate leadership will be instrumental in addressing future challenges. Compassionate leaders will need to balance the demands of technological innovation, regulatory compliance, and sustainability with the core mission of improving patient health and well-being. They will be called upon to make difficult decisions that consider the long-term impacts on patients, employees, communities, and the environment.

By fostering a culture of empathy, ethical conduct, and social responsibility, compassionate leaders can drive positive change and ensure that the pharmaceutical industry continues to meet the needs of patients and society. They will lead by example, demonstrating that business success and compassion are not mutually exclusive, but rather complementary forces that can propel the industry towards a more sustainable and equitable future.

The future of the pharmaceutical industry will be shaped by technological advancements, evolving regulatory landscapes, and increasing emphasis on sustainability and social responsibility. Compassionate leadership will be crucial in navigating these trends and challenges, ensuring that the industry remains focused on its core mission of improving patient health and well-being while also addressing broader societal and environmental concerns.

The Role of Compassionate Leadership in Future Success

Anticipating and Adapting to Technological and Regulatory Changes

Compassionate leadership in the pharmaceutical industry involves a proactive approach to anticipating and adapting to technological and regulatory changes. The rapid pace of technological advancements, such as artificial intelligence (AI), machine learning (ML), and big data analytics, is revolutionizing drug discovery, development, and delivery. Compassionate leaders are those who not only embrace these innovations but also consider their ethical implications. They ensure that technologies are implemented in a manner that maximizes patient benefits while minimizing risks. By fostering an environment that encourages continuous learning and adaptability, these leaders prepare their organizations to stay ahead of the curve, ensuring that they can quickly pivot in response to new regulatory requirements and technological opportunities.

Adapting to regulatory changes is another critical aspect. The pharmaceutical industry faces an increasingly complex and stringent regulatory environment. Compassionate leaders prioritize compliance and ethical conduct, recognizing that regulatory adherence is not merely a bureaucratic hurdle but a commitment to patient safety and public trust. They engage with regulatory bodies transparently and proactively, advocating for patient-centric policies and practices. By embedding a culture of compliance and ethical vigilance within their organizations, compassionate leaders ensure that their companies can navigate regulatory changes smoothly and maintain their license to operate.

Leading with a Focus on Ethical Practices and Social Impact

At the heart of compassionate leadership is a steadfast commitment to ethical practices and social impact. Compassionate leaders understand that their decisions have far-reaching implications for patients, employees, communities, and the environment. They prioritize ethical decision-making processes, ensuring that their companies' actions align with core values of honesty, integrity, and fairness. This focus on ethics fosters a culture of trust and accountability, both internally among employees and externally with stakeholders.

Compassionate leaders also drive their organizations to make a positive social impact. They champion initiatives that address global health challenges, improve access to medications, and enhance the well-being of underserved populations. For example, they may advocate for pricing strategies that make life-saving drugs affordable or support programs that provide free or subsidized medications to those in need. By integrating social responsibility into their business models, compassionate leaders demonstrate that profitability and social good can go hand in hand. This approach not only benefits society but also enhances the company's reputation and long-term sustainability.

Strengthening the Industry's Reputation and Trust Through Compassion-Driven Strategies

Compassionate leadership plays a pivotal role in strengthening the pharmaceutical industry's reputation and building trust. In an industry often scrutinized for high drug prices, ethical lapses, and perceived profit-driven motives, compassionate leaders stand out by prioritizing patient welfare and societal good. They adopt transparency in their operations, openly communicating their strategies, challenges, and successes. This transparency builds trust with patients, healthcare providers, regulators, and the public.

Compassion-driven strategies also involve active engagement with communities and stakeholders. Compassionate leaders listen to the needs and concerns of their stakeholders, incorporating their feedback into decision-making processes. They form strategic partnerships with non-governmental organizations (NGOs), government bodies, and other stakeholders to collaboratively address health challenges. By fostering these partnerships and demonstrating a genuine commitment to societal well-being, compassionate leaders enhance their company's credibility and public trust.

Moreover, compassionate leadership is essential in crisis situations. Leaders who respond to crises with empathy, transparency, and decisive action can mitigate negative impacts and rebuild trust more effectively. For instance, during a drug recall or a public health emergency, a compassionate leader's priority would be to ensure patient safety, communicate clearly with affected parties, and take swift corrective actions. Such a response not only resolves the immediate issue but also strengthens the organization's reputation for integrity and reliability.

Compassionate leadership is critical for the future success of the pharmaceutical industry. By anticipating and adapting to technological and regulatory changes, leading with a focus on ethical practices and social impact, and strengthening the industry's reputation and trust, compassionate leaders ensure that their organizations are not only successful but also respected and trusted by society.

Vision for a Compassionate Future

Imagining the Future of the Pharmaceutical Industry Led by Compassionate Leaders

As we look towards the future, the vision for a pharmaceutical industry guided by compassionate leadership is one of profound transformation and positive impact. In this envisioned future, compassionate leaders prioritize the well-being of patients, employees, and society, creating a ripple effect of benefits that extend beyond the boundaries of their organizations.

Potential Benefits for Employees

1. **Enhanced Workplace Culture**:
   - Compassionate leadership fosters a supportive and inclusive workplace culture where employees feel valued and respected. Leaders who prioritize empathy and understanding create an environment where employees are motivated to perform at their best, leading to higher job satisfaction and lower turnover rates.
   - Such a culture encourages open communication, collaboration, and innovation. Employees are more likely to share ideas and take risks when they feel supported by their leaders, leading to increased creativity and problem-solving capabilities within the organization.
2. **Professional Development and Well-being**:
   - Compassionate leaders invest in the professional development and well-being of their employees. They provide opportunities for continuous learning, skill enhancement, and career growth. This investment not only improves the capabilities of the workforce but also fosters a sense of loyalty and commitment.
   - Additionally, by promoting work-life balance and providing resources for mental and physical health,

compassionate leaders ensure that employees remain healthy, both mentally and physically, reducing burnout and increasing overall productivity.

3. **Ethical and Purpose-Driven Work**:
   - Working under compassionate leaders who prioritize ethical practices and social responsibility gives employees a sense of purpose and pride. Knowing that their work contributes to the greater good and positively impacts society enhances their engagement and motivation.

Potential Benefits for Patients

1. **Patient-Centric Care**:
   - Compassionate leadership places patients at the center of all decision-making processes. This focus leads to the development of patient-centric products and services that address real health needs effectively. By prioritizing patient welfare over profits, pharmaceutical companies can build trust and loyalty among their patient base.
2. **Improved Access to Medications**:
   - Leaders who are driven by compassion work tirelessly to ensure that essential medications are accessible to all, regardless of economic status. This might include implementing tiered pricing strategies, partnering with governments and NGOs to provide subsidies, or investing in programs that deliver free medications to underserved communities.
   - The result is a significant reduction in healthcare disparities and an increase in overall public health. Patients who previously could not afford treatments can now access life-saving medications, leading to improved health outcomes and quality of life.
3. **Transparent and Ethical Practices**:
   - Transparency and ethical practices in clinical trials, drug development, and marketing ensure that patients

are well-informed and confident in the treatments they receive. Compassionate leaders uphold high ethical standards, ensuring that patient safety and rights are always protected.

Potential Benefits for Broader Society

1. **Social Responsibility and Community Engagement**:
    - Compassionate pharmaceutical leaders extend their influence beyond the corporate sphere to actively engage with communities. They invest in community health programs, support local economic development, and partner with public health initiatives to address pressing health issues.
    - These efforts contribute to healthier, more resilient communities. By addressing social determinants of health, such as education, nutrition, and sanitation, pharmaceutical companies can play a crucial role in improving overall societal well-being.
2. **Sustainability and Environmental Stewardship**:
    - In the future, compassionate leaders will also prioritize environmental sustainability. They will implement green practices in manufacturing, reduce waste, and minimize the environmental impact of their operations. This commitment to sustainability not only benefits the planet but also enhances the company's reputation among environmentally conscious consumers and stakeholders.
3. **Ethical Business Practices and Global Impact**:
    - Compassionate leadership sets a standard for ethical business practices that can influence the entire industry. Companies that lead with compassion can drive industry-wide changes, encouraging competitors to adopt similar values and practices.
    - On a global scale, compassionate pharmaceutical leaders can contribute to solving worldwide health challenges, such as pandemics and chronic diseases.

By collaborating with international organizations and sharing knowledge and resources, they can make a significant impact on global health.

The future of the pharmaceutical industry, led by compassionate leaders, is one where the well-being of employees, patients, and society is at the forefront. This vision involves creating supportive and innovative work environments, ensuring patient-centric care and access to medications, and engaging in responsible and ethical business practices that benefit the broader community and the environment. Compassionate leadership has the potential to transform the pharmaceutical industry into a force for good, driving sustainable success and positive change for generations to come.

As we conclude this exploration of leadership in the Indian pharmaceutical industry, it becomes evident that the enduring significance of compassion in leadership cannot be overstated. Compassionate leadership is not just a noble ideal but a critical driver of sustainable success and positive change. By embedding compassion into the core of their leadership approach, leaders can address the multifaceted challenges of the pharmaceutical sector, foster innovation, and build trust with stakeholders.

Compassionate leadership creates an environment where ethical decision-making and social responsibility are paramount. It encourages leaders to view challenges through a human-centered lens, considering the well-being of employees, patients, and communities. This perspective is crucial in an industry that directly impacts public health and safety. Leaders who prioritize compassion are more likely to implement patient-centric practices, ensure equitable access to medications, and maintain the highest ethical standards.

Moreover, compassionate leadership fosters a culture of empathy and support within organizations. Employees who feel valued and understood are more engaged, motivated, and loyal. This, in turn, enhances productivity, reduces turnover, and promotes a collaborative and innovative workplace. Compassionate leaders invest in the professional and personal development of their teams, creating a resilient and adaptive workforce capable of navigating the complexities of the pharmaceutical landscape.

On a broader scale, compassionate leadership can transform the reputation of the pharmaceutical industry. By consistently demonstrating integrity, transparency, and social responsibility, companies can rebuild and strengthen public trust. This trust is essential for long-term success, as it influences consumer behavior, regulatory relationships, and overall market standing. Compassionate leadership, therefore, is not only ethically sound but also strategically advantageous.

As we look to the future, it is imperative for current and aspiring leaders in the Indian pharmaceutical industry to embrace and prioritize compassion in their leadership approach. The challenges and opportunities ahead demand leaders who are not only visionary and innovative but also deeply committed to the well-being of all stakeholders.

Leaders must actively cultivate compassion by fostering an inclusive and supportive organizational culture, prioritizing ethical practices, and engaging with communities in meaningful ways. This commitment to compassion should be reflected in every aspect of their decision-making, from strategic planning to everyday interactions with employees and patients.

The long-term benefits of compassionate leadership extend far beyond immediate business outcomes. By leading with compassion, pharmaceutical companies can drive significant improvements in public health, contribute to societal well-being, and inspire positive change within the industry. The ripple effect of compassionate leadership has the potential to create a more just, equitable, and healthy society.

In conclusion, the journey towards sustainable success in the Indian pharmaceutical industry is intrinsically linked to the principles of compassionate leadership. By embedding compassion into the fabric of their organizations, leaders can navigate challenges with resilience, foster innovation, and build enduring trust with stakeholders. Let this book serve as a guide and inspiration for leaders to prioritize compassion, recognizing its profound impact on the industry and society at large. Embrace compassion, and lead with integrity, and together, we can shape a brighter future for the Indian pharmaceutical sector and the world.

Verses Kindler Publication

Verses Kindler Publication

Reach us through our website -
https://www.verseskindlerpublication.com/
For more information visit our Instagram or Facebook page.

9 789356 058446

Printed at Repro India Ltd.